A 30-Day Guide to Healing and

Building Self-Worth

Workbook

Author: Pearl Truesdale

Self-Published. Printed in the USA.

For more information, please contact at:

journeysofwomenministries@gmail.com

Website: www.journeysofwomenministries.net

Digital ISBN# 979-8-9914878-2-5

Paperback ISBN# 979-8-9914878-3-2

Dedicated to:

The Father, The Son, and The Holy Spirit.

May this guide plant seeds of healing and growth:

To all God's Children

The Healing and Growth Collection: 30-Day Guide Series

Welcome to *The Healing and Growth Collection, 30-Day Guide Series*. This series is designed to empower women as they navigate the complex journey of healing from past trauma and abuse. Each book or eBook in the collection offers a unique opportunity to heal at your own pace, providing a safe and nurturing space crafted by someone who truly understands your struggles. To enhance your experience and support your healing process, a *Healing Journal* is available with each book or eBook. The journal serves as a companion, offering guided reflections and personal writing exercises to help you deepen your growth and track your progress as you journey through healing.

This collection is the work of Pearl Truesdale, a survivor, and victor of mental, physical and sexual abuse. Pearl's journey through pain and recovery has fueled her passion for helping other women find their paths to healing. She has dedicated her life to offering guidance, support, and hope to those who face the daunting task of overcoming the scars left by abuse. In this series, you will find the tools, encouragement, and wisdom needed to confront the challenges that may arise on your healing journey. Pearl understands the fear, uncertainty, and pain that accompany such a journey, and she is here to walk alongside you every step of the way.

You are not alone—Pearl the founder of Journeys of Women Ministries is here to support you as you reclaim your strength, rebuild your life, and move forward with courage and hope. Pearl, a motivational Christian speaker, is an inspiring example of resilience and strength. Through her own experiences of overcoming trauma from past abuse, she has emerged as a beacon of hope for others facing similar challenges.

In her book, "Hope Victory Over Darkness," Pearl courageously shares her journey, providing valuable insights and practical strategies for healing. As a podcaster, she continues to reach a wider audience, spreading messages of empowerment and encouragement. By creating these eBooks and online courses, Pearl demonstrates her commitment to supporting and assisting women in their own healing journeys, offering a safe space for reflection, growth, and transformation.

As a course creator, Pearl draws upon her own experiences to develop a curriculum that is both comprehensive and compassionate. By weaving together her personal story with evidence-based practices, she ensures that the course offers a holistic approach to healing from past abuse. Through a combination of storytelling, reflection exercises, and practical tools, students are guided towards a deeper understanding of their own experiences and empowered to reclaim their sense of self-worth and agency. Pearl's multifaceted approach not only educates but also inspires, creating a supportive environment where women can find the strength and courage to overcome their trauma and step into a brighter, more hopeful future.

ABOUT: Pearl Truesdale

PASSIONATE ADVOCATE FOR SEXUAL ABUSE & RAPE VICTIMS

Pearl was adopted into the arms of a pedophile at the tender age of four years old. Her adopted mother would leave her every morning with her adopted father to prep and groom her. Pearl's adopted mother died a year and a half later, leaving her vulnerable to the clutches of her abuser for the next four thousand days and nights.

During those long days and nights of mental, physical, and sexual abuse, she would receive moments of truth and knowledge to help her to hold on one more day. As a young teenager she escaped her adopted father's abuse thinking she was saved and free from her pain, but little did she know that she would be put into the same scenario she had left but only different people. She would run away trying to find her freedom just to walk the streets, living in cars or wherever she could. She was tried to find her happiness, but something was missing. She did not know what happiness was. Her mind was confused, lost, and alone.

She faced unimaginable trauma and abuse at a tender age. Despite the pain and suffering that seemed never-ending, Pearl displayed incredible strength and resilience. Her ability to endure such hardships and never give up is a testament to the unyielding spirit within her. Through her story, we can learn the power of perseverance in the face of adversity and the importance of holding onto hope even in the darkest of times. Pearl's journey serves as a reminder that no matter how challenging life may get, there is always a glimmer of light at the end of the tunnel if we choose to keep moving forward.

This is why she has built Journeys of Women Ministries to help women of all ages, ethnicities, and backgrounds overcome the trauma from past abuse. She understands the weight that past experiences can carry and the impact they can have on your well-being. Through this Ministry, her goal is to create a safe space where you can heal, grow, and reclaim your power. Together, we will work towards healing old wounds, building resilience, and embracing a future filled with hope and possibility. Remember, you are not alone on this journey, and support is always available to help you thrive once again.

We are all beautiful souls!

TABLE OF CONTENTS

Chapter 1: Days 1-7

Embracing Your Journey:

Finding Strength in Every Step Forward

Chapter 2: Days 8-14

Rewriting Your Inner Dialogue:

Overcoming Negative Self-Talk and Building Confidence

Chapter 3: Days 15-21

Building Resilience Through Self Worth:

Strengthening Your Foundation for Lasting Change

Chapter 4: Days 22-30

New Steps: What Is Yours?

Charting Your Path Forward

Chapter 1

Embracing Your Journey

Finding Strength in Every Step Forward

Days 1-7: Recognizing Your Strengths

The first step in any journey is often the hardest, but it is also the most significant. In this chapter, we begin the process of healing by recognizing and celebrating the strengths you have gained along the way. Healing is not a linear process, and it starts with acknowledging the progress you've already made. These first seven days will help you look inward, reflecting on your journey thus far, and uncovering the resilience that has brought you to this moment.

As you reflect on your past, you'll see how each experience, both good and bad, has shaped your character and built your inner strength. This chapter invites you to take time to acknowledge your own courage and growth, finding empowerment in the small but steady steps forward. Remember that embracing your journey with compassion and self-awareness is key to continuing your path toward healing and building self-worth. Each reflection will help you gain deeper insight into the unique strengths you carry and how they can propel you toward the future you desire.

Understanding Your Journey begins with taking a moment to reflect on your current emotional state and where you are in your journey. Healing starts with awareness, and understanding where you stand emotionally allows you to acknowledge the areas where growth and healing are needed. It's important to give yourself permission to feel whatever emotions come up without judgment—whether it's fear, sadness, or uncertainty. Recognizing these emotions is the first step in understanding how your past experiences have shaped the way you view yourself and your current path. By being honest with yourself, you open the door to deeper self-awareness, which is key to building a foundation for healing and self-worth. As ***Psalm 46:1-2*** reminds us, ***"God is our*** *refuge and strength, an ever-present help in trouble. Therefore we will not fear, though the earth give way and the mountains fall into the heart of the sea."* In moments of reflection, trust that God is your refuge, giving you the strength to face your emotions and begin healing.

As you reflect on your journey, consider the path you've been on and the experiences that have brought you to this moment. What challenges have you faced, and how have they influenced your emotional state? Understanding your past can help you identify patterns, both positive and negative, that have impacted your sense of self. This is not about reliving painful moments but rather about gaining insight into how your emotions and experiences have shaped your journey so far. *Psalm 46:1-2* serves as a reminder that even when everything around you feels uncertain or overwhelming, God is your ever-present help. He provides the strength you need to navigate this process with courage and resilience. Take time to reflect, write, and embrace the process of understanding your journey more deeply.

Weekly Prayer for Chapter 1: Embracing Your Journey

Heavenly Father,

As I embark on this journey of healing, I ask for Your strength and guidance each day. Help me to recognize the strength You've placed within me and to embrace vulnerability as a path to deeper growth. Let each step I take be filled with Your grace, and may I trust in Your plan even when I cannot see the full picture. Teach me to celebrate my progress, however small, and to trust in the process of healing. Thank You for walking beside me, giving me the courage to move forward with faith, resilience, and self-worth.

In Jesus' name, I pray. Amen.

Workbook Lessons Week 1

Embracing Your Journey

Finding Strength in Every Step Forward

Welcome to Chapter 1, where your journey toward healing and self-worth begins by recognizing your strengths and acknowledging the path you've traveled so far. Over the next seven days, we will reflect on key areas that shape your emotional and spiritual growth, guiding you to embrace the challenges you've faced and find strength in every step you take forward.

Each day in this lesson is designed to encourage deeper self-awareness, inviting you to reflect on your current emotional state, open yourself to vulnerability, and celebrate the progress you've made. Through this chapter, you will learn to trust the process of healing and growth, allowing small steps to make a big impact. Whether you're facing the fear of failure or learning to trust God's plan even when it's not immediately visible, these seven days will help you establish a foundation for the rest of your journey.

By the end of the week, you'll be empowered to set personal healing goals, recognizing that each moment of self-reflection and intention brings you closer to becoming the person you're meant to be. This chapter is not just about looking back but about moving forward with confidence, faith, and a renewed sense of self-worth. Let's begin this powerful journey, one step at a time.

<u>Workbook Lesson: Day 1 – Understanding Your Journey</u>

Reflect on Your Current Emotional State and the Path You Are On

Reflecting on your current emotional state is the first step in understanding where you are on your healing journey. It's important to take time to acknowledge your feelings—whether they are of peace, anxiety, sadness, or joy. Recognizing these emotions allows you to see how they are shaped by your past experiences and influences your present actions. As **Psalm 139:23-24** (NIV) reminds us, ***"Search me, God, and know my heart; test me and know my anxious thoughts. See if there is any offensive way in me, and lead me in the way everlasting."*** This invitation to self-reflection encourages you to be honest with your emotions and trust that God is with you as you uncover deeper layers of your heart and mind.

As you reflect on your emotional state, consider the path you've traveled. What challenges have you faced, and how have they shaped who you are today? It's important to remember that this reflection is not about reliving painful moments but about gaining insight into how your past influences your present. By understanding these connections, you create space for growth, healing, and transformation. *Proverbs 4:23* (NIV) teaches us, ***"Above all else, guard your heart, for everything you do flows from it."*** In recognizing where you are emotionally, you can better protect your heart and guide it toward healing and restoration.

Purpose:

The purpose of this lesson is to guide you in reflecting on your current emotional state and understanding where you are in your journey. This reflection is the foundation for healing and growth, as it helps you become aware of your emotions, experiences, and the path you have taken to reach this point.

Introduction:

Understanding your journey begins with acknowledging your present emotional state. Healing starts with awareness, and by taking time to reflect on how you feel today, you can begin to understand the deeper emotions driving your actions and responses. This lesson invites you to look inward without judgment, giving yourself permission to experience the full range of emotions that surface. Whether it's fear, sadness, joy, or uncertainty, each emotion has shaped your path and contributes to the next step forward. By being present with your feelings and recognizing the impact of past experiences, you create a space for healing, self-compassion, and transformation.

Reflection Exercise:

1. **Identify Your Current Emotional State:** Take a few moments to reflect on your feelings right now. How would you describe your emotional state in one or two words?

Journal Prompt: Write down what comes to mind—whether it's peaceful, anxious, excited, or overwhelmed. There's no right or wrong answer, only the truth of how you feel in this moment.

_____

_____

_____

2. **Connect Emotions with Your Journey:** As you reflect, consider how your current emotions connect to past experiences. Are there patterns from your past that continue to affect your emotional state today?

    Journal Prompt: Write down any events or memories that feel relevant to your present emotions and consider how these have shaped your journey up to this point.

_____

_____

_____

3. **Recognize the Opportunity for Growth:** Acknowledge that the emotions you feel today are part of your healing journey. Understanding your emotional state is a powerful step toward growth.

   Journal Prompt: Write down one way in which being aware of your emotions can help guide your next steps on this path.

   _____

   _____

   _____

Reflection Question:

How does recognizing and reflecting on your current emotional state help you gain greater insight into your healing journey, and how can you use this awareness to move forward with compassion for yourself?

   Journal Prompt: Write down a few sentences your current state of mind helps you gain insight into you healing journal and how can you use it to help you move forward.

_____

_____

_____

Day – 1 Conclusion: Embracing Self-Awareness: A Courageous First Step

As you conclude Day 1 of your journey, take a moment to honor the courage it took to reflect on your current emotional state. Acknowledging your feelings, whether they are peaceful or difficult, is a powerful step in understanding where you are and where you're headed. This reflection offers you the opportunity to connect with your inner self and recognize how past experiences have shaped your emotions today. By bringing these emotions to light, you are not only gaining clarity but also creating space for healing and growth. As you move forward, remember that this awareness is a tool you can use to guide yourself with compassion, grace, and understanding. Today marks the beginning of a journey toward greater self-awareness, healing, and transformation.

Workbook Lesson: Day 2 – Embracing Vulnerability

Explore How Embracing Vulnerability Helps You Grow Stronger

Embracing vulnerability is often seen as a daunting task, but it is one of the most powerful ways to grow stronger. Vulnerability invites us to open ourselves up, share our fears, and express our pain. Rather than being a sign of weakness, it is a testament to courage and resilience. In *2 Corinthians 12:9*, God reminds us, *"My grace is sufficient for you, for my power is made perfect in weakness."* This verse teaches us that when we embrace our vulnerability, we allow God's strength to shine through. In our moments of weakness, God's grace uplifts and empowers us, transforming vulnerability into a source of strength and healing.

Through vulnerability, we also develop deeper connections with ourselves, others, and God. When we allow ourselves to be seen as we truly are—flaws, fears, and all—we create space for authentic relationships to flourish. Vulnerability fosters empathy and trust, encouraging others to embrace their own stories of growth and healing. By sharing our struggles and leaning into vulnerability, we build stronger emotional and spiritual bonds, which in turn deepen our faith and resilience.

Purpose:

The purpose of this lesson is to help you understand the importance of vulnerability as a pathway to personal growth. By embracing vulnerability, you allow yourself to experience deeper healing, build meaningful connections with others, and strengthen your emotional resilience.

Introduction:

Vulnerability can often feel intimidating, as it requires you to open up and expose parts of yourself that you may have kept hidden—your fears, insecurities, and pain. However, vulnerability is not a sign of weakness; rather, it is a source of true strength. As you learn to embrace your vulnerabilities, you also embrace your authenticity, allowing yourself to grow in ways that would not be possible without openness.

In *Matthew 11:28-30*, Jesus invites us to come to Him with our burdens and weariness, promising rest and peace in return. Vulnerability is an act of trust, where we allow ourselves to lean into God's grace and love, knowing that we don't have to carry everything on our own. Through vulnerability, you will discover that you are not alone, and by sharing your true self, you will grow stronger in your faith, relationships, and personal healing journey.

Reflection Exercise:

1. **Identify Vulnerabilities:** Take a few minutes to reflect on areas of your life where you feel vulnerable. What

fears or insecurities have you been carrying that you've been afraid to express?

Journal Prompt: Write down these vulnerabilities and acknowledge how they have affected your life.

_____

_____

_____

2. **Reframe Vulnerability as Strength:** Think about how vulnerability can be an opportunity for growth. How can embracing your vulnerability make you stronger?

   Journal Prompt: Write down one way you can shift your mindset to see vulnerability as a positive force for healing and connection in your life.

_____

_____

_____

3. **Practice Vulnerability:** Choose one area of your life where you can practice vulnerability this week. Whether it's having an honest conversation with someone,

   expressing your true feelings or sharing your story with someone you trust.

   Journal Prompt: Write down how you will take this step.

   _____

   _____

   _____

Reflection Question:

How can embracing vulnerability in your personal journey help you grow stronger and deepen your relationships with God and others?

   Journal Prompt: Write about a time when being vulnerable led to growth in your life and consider how you can embrace vulnerability moving forward.

_____

_____

_____

Day 2 – Conclusion: The Strength in Openness: Embracing Vulnerability for Growth

As you conclude Day 2, take a moment to reflect on the strength you've found in embracing vulnerability. By opening yourself up and sharing your fears or insecurities, you've taken a courageous step toward personal growth and healing. Vulnerability is not a weakness but a powerful testament to your resilience and trust in God's grace. As *2 Corinthians 12:9* reminds us, His power is made perfect in our weakness, and through vulnerability, we allow His strength to shine through us. Moving forward, continue to lean into this openness, knowing that each time you embrace vulnerability, you build deeper connections with yourself, others, and God, fostering greater healing and emotional resilience.

Workbook Lesson: Day 3 – Small Steps, Big Impact

Learn How Small Changes Lead to Significant Growth

Small changes, though they may seem insignificant at first, can lead to profound growth over time. The key to lasting transformation is often found in the consistent practice of small, positive actions that, when accumulated, create a ripple effect. In *Zechariah 4:10* (NLT), we are reminded, ***"Do not despise these small beginnings, for the Lord rejoices to see the work begin."*** This scripture emphasizes that even the smallest of efforts are valued and can lead to great results when pursued with faith and persistence. Whether it's setting aside a few minutes for reflection, practicing gratitude, or making intentional choices in your daily life, these small steps build the foundation for significant personal growth.

As we focus on small, steady improvements, we cultivate resilience and a sense of accomplishment that drives us forward. Growth doesn't always happen in grand gestures or dramatic moments; it unfolds gradually as we remain committed to the process. Each small step, whether emotional, spiritual, or practical, is part of a larger journey toward healing and self-worth. By celebrating these small victories, we reinforce the belief that change is possible, and that we are actively shaping a brighter, more empowered future, one step at a time.

Purpose:

The purpose of this lesson is to help you recognize that growth doesn't happen overnight. By focusing on small, consistent steps, you can achieve significant transformations over time. This lesson will guide you to understand how each small action contributes to your overall progress and healing journey.

Introduction:

Growth often seems daunting when we focus only on the big picture. However, significant transformations are the result of small, intentional steps taken over time. In *Zechariah 4:10* (NLT), we are reminded, *"Do not despise these small beginnings, for the Lord rejoices to see the work begin."* This scripture teaches us that no step is too small when it is part of a larger journey of healing and self-worth.

The impact of small, steady efforts can be far greater than we initially realize. Whether it's establishing a daily habit, shifting a mindset, or celebrating a small win, each action builds upon the last, creating a ripple effect that leads to significant personal growth. As you work through this lesson, you will learn to appreciate the value of small steps and how thcy contribute to long-lasting transformation.

Reflection Exercise:

1. **Identify Your Small Steps:** Take a moment to reflect on small changes you've made recently that have contributed to your personal growth. It could be as simple as starting a new morning routine, expressing gratitude more often, or setting a small boundary.

   Journal Prompt: Write down at least two small steps that you have taken.

_____

_____

_____

2. **Recognize the Impact:** Reflect on how these small actions have already impacted your life. What benefits have you noticed? How have these small changes made you feel more confident or empowered?

   Journal Prompt: Write down the positive effects you've experienced as a result of these small actions.

_____

_____

_____

3. **Set a New Small Step:** Think about one new small step you can implement in your life that aligns with your healing journey. It might be setting aside five minutes for

4. meditation, sending a message of gratitude to someone, or tackling a simple task you've been avoiding.

Journal Prompt: Write down your new small step and commit to practicing it daily for the next week.

_____

_____

_____

Reflection Question:

How have small steps contributed to your growth in the past, and what small changes can you make now to continue moving forward in your healing journey?

Journal Prompt: Write about the impact of small actions in your life and how you can remain consistent in taking steps toward growth.

_____

_____

_____

Day 3 – Conclusion: The Power of Small Steps: Embracing Steady Progress

As you conclude Day 3, take a moment to appreciate the significance of the small steps you've taken so far. Each small action, though it may seem minor at first, is a building block in your journey toward growth and healing. *Zechariah 4:10* reminds us that even the smallest of beginnings are valuable in the eyes of God, and your consistent efforts are shaping a brighter, more empowered future. By focusing on these small, steady improvements, you're cultivating resilience and momentum that will lead to profound transformation over time. Remember, every small step counts, and with each one, you are moving closer to the person you are becoming.

Workbook Lesson: Day 4 – Overcoming Fear of Failure

Focus on How Fear Holds You Back and How to Move Beyond It

Fear often acts as an invisible barrier, preventing us from pursuing growth, healing, and new opportunities. It can manifest as self-doubt, hesitation, or avoidance, holding us back from reaching our full potential. When fear takes over, it convinces us to stay in our comfort zones, where we feel safe but stagnant. However, moving beyond fear requires recognizing its presence and understanding that it's a natural part of growth. By facing our fears head-on, we begin to dismantle the power they hold over us. Taking small, courageous steps forward, even in the face of uncertainty, helps us build confidence and resilience. Each time we choose to act despite fear, we reclaim control and move closer to the life we are meant to live.

Purpose:

The purpose of this lesson is to help you recognize how the fear of failure holds you back from growth and healing. By addressing this fear and learning strategies to move beyond it, you will be empowered to embrace progress, even in the face of challenges and setbacks.

Introduction:

Fear of failure is a common barrier to growth, often preventing us from taking the steps necessary for healing and self-improvement. This fear can paralyze us, keeping us in our comfort zones and stopping us from moving forward. However, failure is not a sign of weakness, but an essential part of the growth process. In fact, it's through our mistakes and struggles that we learn, adapt, and become stronger.

Scripture reminds us of this truth in ***Isaiah 41:10*** (NIV), where God says, ***"So do not fear, for I am with you; do not be dismayed, for I am your God. I will strengthen you and help you; I will uphold you with my righteous right hand."*** With God's strength, we can confront our fears and understand that failure is not final. By shifting our perspective on failure, we can view it as an opportunity for growth, learning, and greater resilience.

Reflection Exercise:

1. **Identify Your Fears:** Reflect on areas of your life where fear of failure has held you back. What specific goals or opportunities have you avoided because of this fear?

   Journal Prompt: Write down two or three examples where fear of failure has prevented you from moving forward.

   _____

   _____

   _____

2. **Reframe Your Perspective:** Consider how you can change your perspective on failure. Instead of seeing it as something to avoid, view it as a steppingstone toward growth and self-discovery. Think of a time when a setback or mistake taught you something valuable.

Journal Prompt: Write about how that experience contributed to your personal growth.

_____

_____

_____

3. **Take a Step Forward:** Choose one area where fear of failure has been holding you back and decide to take a small step forward despite that fear. It could be trying something new, setting a boundary, or taking on a task you've been avoiding.

   Journal Prompt: Write down the step you're committing to taking and how you'll encourage yourself to follow through.

_____

_____

_____

Reflection Question:

In what ways has the fear of failure held you back, and how can you begin to shift your perspective to see failure as a valuable part of your growth journey?

Journal Prompt: Write about how you can embrace failure as a necessary step toward success and healing.

_____ _____

_____

_____

Day 4 – Conclusion: Overcoming Fear: Embracing Growth Beyond Failure

As you conclude Day 4, take a moment to acknowledge the courage it takes to face your fear of failure. Recognizing how fear has held you back is the first step toward breaking free from its grip. Today, you've reflected on the ways in which fear has kept you in your comfort zone, preventing you from reaching your full potential. By shifting your perspective and seeing failure as a valuable part of growth, you are opening yourself up to new possibilities. Remember, each step forward, no matter how small, is a victory over fear. With every courageous action, you move closer to the life you desire, filled with resilience, strength, and healing.

Workbook Lesson: Day 5 – Celebrating Progress

Take Time to Celebrate the Steps You've Already Taken

Taking time to celebrate the steps you've already taken is an essential part of the healing and growth process. Often, we focus so much on what lies ahead that we forget to acknowledge how far we've come. Every small victory, every moment of progress, deserves recognition. Celebrating these milestones not only boosts your confidence but also reinforces the positive changes you're making in your life. It reminds you that growth is happening, even if it feels slow or unsteady at times. By pausing to appreciate your journey, you cultivate gratitude and motivation, empowering yourself to continue moving forward with renewed energy and purpose.

Purpose:

The purpose of this lesson is to encourage you to pause and reflect on the progress you've made so far in your healing journey. By acknowledging and celebrating your growth, you can build motivation, confidence, and gratitude for the steps you've already taken.

Introduction:

In the midst of any journey, it's easy to focus on what still needs to be done rather than what has already been accomplished. However, recognizing and celebrating even small victories is essential to maintaining momentum and fostering self-worth. Celebrating progress doesn't mean the journey is over, but it helps you see how far you've come and reinforces the positive changes you're making in your life.

Scripture encourages us to celebrate progress as we grow, as seen in ***Philippians 1:6*** (NIV): ***"Being confident of this, that he who began a good work in you will carry it on to completion until the day of Christ Jesus."*** God is at work in you, and every step, no matter how small, is a part of that work. By taking time to acknowledge your progress, you remind yourself that healing is a process, and each moment of growth is worth celebrating.

Reflection Exercise:

1. **Reflect on Your Journey:** Take a few minutes to think about where you started and where you are now. What are the significant changes, big or small, that you've experienced since you began this journey?

   Journal Prompt: Write down at least three specific areas where you have made progress, whether emotionally, spiritually, or physically.

_____

_____

_____

2. **Celebrate Small Wins:** It's easy to overlook small victories, but they are just as important as the larger milestones. Reflect on the small changes you've made—such as a shift in mindset, healthier responses to triggers, or a growing sense of inner peace—and take time to celebrate these.

   Journal Prompt: Write down how these small steps have contributed to your overall healing.

_____

_____

_____

3. **Plan a Celebration:** To truly honor your progress, plan a small celebration for yourself. It could be something as simple as taking a walk in nature, treating yourself to a

favorite activity, or writing a letter of gratitude to yourself.

Journal Prompt: Write down how you plan to celebrate your progress today and what this celebration means to you.

_____

_____

_____

Reflection Question:

How does recognizing and celebrating the steps you've already taken encourage you to keep moving forward on your healing journey?

Journal Prompt: Write about how celebrating progress impacts your motivation and sense of self-worth.

_____

_____

_____

Day 5 – Conclusion: Celebrating Progress: Embracing Growth with Gratitude

As you conclude Day 5, take a moment to reflect on and celebrate the progress you've made so far. Every small victory, no matter how minor it may seem, is a testament to your growth and resilience. By acknowledging these steps, you remind yourself that healing is not about perfection but about continual progress. *Philippians 1:6* encourages us to trust in the work God is doing within us, knowing that He will carry it on to completion. By celebrating your progress, you cultivate gratitude, boost your confidence, and reinforce the positive changes you're making in your life. Let these moments of reflection inspire and motivate you to keep moving forward with renewed purpose and energy.

Workbook Lesson: Day 6 – Trusting the Process

Learn to Have Faith in Your Journey, Even When You Don't See Immediate Results

Learning to have faith in your journey, especially when immediate results aren't visible, is one of the most challenging but rewarding aspects of personal growth. It requires trust in the process and a deep belief that the small steps you're taking will eventually lead to significant transformation. When progress seems slow or invisible, it can be easy to become discouraged, but it's important to remember that growth often happens beneath the surface, much like the roots of a tree before it sprouts above ground. In these moments, leaning into faith becomes a crucial part of your journey, reminding you that every step, no matter how small, is leading you closer to your goals.

As *Galatians 6:9* (NIV) encourages, *"Let us not become weary in doing good, for at the proper time we will reap a harvest if we do not give up. "* This verse is a reminder that persistence and patience are essential virtues on the path to healing and growth. Even when you cannot yet see the fruits of your efforts, trust that they are coming. Faith in the journey allows you to move forward with hope and confidence, knowing that the work you are putting in today will eventually result in the transformation you seek. Keep going, and trust that your efforts are not in vain.

Purpose:

The purpose of this lesson is to help you develop trust in the journey of healing, even when progress seems slow or results are not immediately visible. By learning to have faith in the process, you will cultivate patience, resilience, and the understanding that growth takes time.

Introduction:

Healing is not a linear path. There will be times when progress feels slow, or you may feel like you're not moving forward at all. But just as a plant grows roots before sprouting above the soil, significant growth often happens beneath the surface.

Trusting the process requires faith that every step, every effort, and every moment of reflection is contributing to your healing and growth, even if the results are not immediately apparent.

Scripture reminds us again to trust in God's timing and process. ***Galatians 6:9*** (NIV) says: ***"Let us not become weary in doing good, for at the proper time we will reap a harvest if we do not give up."*** This verse encourages us to remain steadfast and patient, knowing that the fruits of our journey will come in time. Your healing, much like a harvest, requires nurturing, patience, and trust in the process.

Reflection Exercise:

1. **Reflect on Times of Waiting:** Take a moment to think about previous times in your life when you had to wait for something important—whether it was personal growth, a change in circumstances, or an answer to a prayer. How did that waiting period affect you, and what did you learn from it?

Journal Prompt: Write down at least one experience where waiting and trusting the process led to eventual growth or insight.

_____

_____

_____

2. **Identify Areas of Uncertainty:** Think about areas in your current healing journey where you feel uncertain or frustrated by the lack of visible results. Write down these areas and reflect on how you can shift your mindset from impatience to trust.

   Journal Prompt: Consider and write down how you can release the need for immediate outcomes and instead focus on the steps you are taking each day.

_____

_____

_____

3. **Affirming Trust:** To reinforce your trust in the process, write an affirmation or prayer that you can repeat daily. It could be something like: *"I trust that God is guiding my journey, and I have faith that every step I take is moving me toward healing."*

   Journal Prompt: Write down your affirmation and commit to saying it whenever doubts arise.

   _____

   _____

   _____

Reflection Question:

How does trusting the process change the way you view your healing journey, and what steps can you take to cultivate more faith and patience as you continue moving forward?

   Journal Prompt: Write about the areas in your life where trust needs to grow, and how you can embrace the journey with greater faith.

_____

_____

_____

Day 6 – Conclusion: Trusting the Journey: Embracing Patience and Faith

As you conclude Day 6, take comfort in knowing that trusting the process is an integral part of your healing journey. Even when results seem distant or progress feels slow, remember that every step you take is leading you closer to transformation. Like a tree that grows its roots before breaking through the surface, your growth may not always be visible, but it is happening beneath the surface. *Galatians 6:9* reminds us not to grow weary in doing good, for at the proper time, you will reap a harvest if you do not give up. Keep faith in the journey, trust that your efforts are not in vain, and embrace the patience required for lasting change.

Workbook Lesson: Day 7 – Setting Your Healing Goals

Define What Healing Looks Like for You and Set Intentions for the Rest of the Journey

Defining what healing looks like for you is a deeply personal process, as it varies from person to person. Healing may mean emotional freedom, forgiveness, self-acceptance, or the ability to move forward without the weight of past traumas. Take a moment to reflect on what healing truly means for you in this season of your life. It might involve letting go of old wounds, building healthier relationships, or rediscovering your sense of purpose. By taking the time to define your version of healing, you provide yourself with a clear vision of what you are working toward, which will help guide your steps moving forward.

Setting intentions for the rest of your journey is about creating small, achievable goals that align with your definition of healing. These intentions will help you stay focused and motivated, giving you direction as you continue to grow. Whether it's committing to self-care, learning new coping mechanisms, or building stronger spiritual practices, your intentions serve as a roadmap for your healing journey. As you move forward, allow these intentions to evolve and grow with you, offering a sense of purpose and clarity as you work toward becoming the best version of yourself.

Purpose:

The purpose of this lesson is to guide you in defining what healing means for you personally and to help you set clear intentions for the rest of your healing journey. By identifying your unique goals, you can approach your healing with purpose and direction, ensuring that each step you take is aligned with your vision of growth.

Introduction:

Healing is a deeply personal journey, and what healing looks like for one person may be different for another. On this day, you are invited to reflect on your personal definition of healing. This is not about reaching perfection or "fixing" yourself—it's about growth, self-acceptance, and emotional freedom. Setting healing goals allows you to take ownership of your journey, guiding you with clear intentions and helping you track your progress along the way.

Think about what healing would mean for you in practical, emotional, and spiritual terms. Is it freedom from certain fears? Releasing past hurts? Cultivating self-compassion? ***Philippians 3:13-14*** (NIV) reminds us***: "Forgetting what is behind and straining toward what is ahead, I press on toward the goal to win the prize for which God has called me heavenward in Christ Jesus."*** As you move forward, focus on the future you are creating, pressing forward with hope and intention.

Reflection Exercise:

1. **Visualize Your Healing:** Close your eyes and take a moment to imagine what your life would look like when you feel healed and whole. What emotions are present? What aspects of your life are different? What relationships or behaviors have shifted?

Journal Prompt: Write down this vision of your healed self, describing it as vividly as possible.

_____

_____

_____

2. **Define Your Healing Goals:** Based on your vision of healing, create a list of 2-3 specific goals you want to work toward during the rest of this journey. These could be emotional goals (such as letting go of resentment), spiritual goals (like deepening your faith), or practical goals (such as establishing healthy boundaries).

   Journal Prompt: Be honest with yourself and write down about what you need and desire in your healing process.

_____

_____

_____

3. **Set Your Intentions:** These steps don't have to be grand or complicated—sometimes the smallest actions can lead to the biggest breakthroughs. Setting these intentions will give you direction and focus as you continue your healing journey.

   Journal Prompt: Write down one small action step you can take toward each goal over the next week.

   _____

   _____

   _____

Reflection Question:

What does healing mean to you personally, and how can setting clear goals and intentions help you stay focused and committed to your journey?

   Journal Prompt: Write about how your healing goals align with the vision of your future self and how they will shape your next steps forward.

_____

_____

_____

Day 7 – Conclusion: Creating Your Path: Defining Personal Healing and Growth

As you conclude Day 7, take a moment to reflect on the clarity you've gained in defining what healing looks like for you. By setting specific goals and intentions, you have crafted a personal roadmap that will guide your journey forward. Remember, healing is not a one-size-fits-all process; it's deeply personal and shaped by your own experiences, emotions, and desires for growth. *Philippians 3:13-14* reminds us to let go of what is behind and to press forward with hope and determination, trusting that each step will bring us closer to the future we envision. You've taken meaningful steps in shaping your path, and each goal you set is another layer of foundation for your emotional freedom and spiritual growth.

As you continue, be mindful that healing is a gradual journey, and it's important to celebrate even the smallest milestones along the way. By staying committed to your vision and setting achievable goals, you are making progress toward becoming the best version of yourself—one rooted in self-compassion and strength. Trust in this process, knowing that every step forward is a testament to your resilience and determination. Keep pressing on, with faith that God is guiding you toward a place of peace and wholeness.

Activity:

"Strength in Every Step"

Reflection and Commitment

Objective:

This activity is designed to help you reflect on your healing journey throughout Week 1 and to set a firm foundation for the next steps forward. By taking time to acknowledge your growth, embrace your vulnerabilities, and celebrate small victories, you will build momentum and confidence as you continue your path to healing and self-worth.

Materials Needed:

- Journal or notebook

- Pen

- A quiet, comfortable space

- Optional: A small object or token (such as a stone, coin, or item of personal significance) to symbolize your healing journey

---

Step 1: Reflection on the Journey So Far (15 minutes)

Find a quiet space where you won't be interrupted. Bring your journal and sit comfortably. Take a few deep breaths, allowing yourself to center and be fully present in this moment. Reflect on your emotional state from the beginning of the week to now. How have your feelings shifted? What insights have surfaced about your strengths, vulnerabilities, or fears?

In your journal, write a brief summary of each day's reflection from this week:

Day 1: What did you learn about your current emotional state and the path you are on?

Journal Prompt:

_____

_____

_____

Day 2: How did embracing vulnerability help you recognize areas of strength?

Journal Prompt:

_____

_____

_____

Day 3: What small steps have had a significant impact on your healing journey?

Journal Prompt:

_____

_____

_____

Day 4: How have you begun to overcome the fear of failure and move beyond it?

Journal Prompt:

_____

_____

_____

Day 5: What progress have you celebrated, and how has this affected your motivation?

Journal Prompt:

_____

_____

_____

Day 6: What have you learned about trusting the process of healing, even without immediate results?

Journal Prompt:

_____

_____

_____

Day 7: How will these intentions of setting goals guide you through the next stages of your journey, and what will success feel like as you reach these milestones?

Journal Prompt:

_____

_____

_____

Step 2: Commit to Your Next Step (10 minutes)

After reflecting on your progress, it's time to set your intentions for the week ahead. In this step, you will focus on creating a commitment that aligns with the healing goals and intentions you've set on Day 7.

Journal Prompt: Write down 1-2 specific intentions or goals that you want to work on moving forward. These should be achievable, actionable steps that help you stay on track in your journey. Consider what emotional or spiritual practices will support you, such as prayer, journaling, or meditation.

_____

_____

_____

Step 3: Symbol of Commitment (5 minutes)

Hold the object you chose (the stone, coin, or other token) in your hand. Close your eyes and imagine this object as a representation of your healing journey. Every time you hold or look at this object, let it remind you of the strength you've found in every step forward.

Now, make a personal commitment to yourself, such as: *"I commit to continuing this journey with patience, self-compassion, and trust. Every step forward is a victory, and I am moving toward healing, strength, and self-worth."*

Journal Prompt: Write your commitment down in your journal and place the object somewhere visible in your space as a daily reminder.

_____

_____

_____

Step 4: Celebrate Progress (5 minutes)

Finally, celebrate the work you've done this week! Take a moment to feel proud of the effort you've put into your healing. Whether you've uncovered new emotions, embraced vulnerability, or made small steps forward, each day has brought you closer to the person you are becoming. Consider treating yourself to a small celebration—a favorite activity, a moment of relaxation, or a quiet moment of gratitude.

Reflection Question:

How has reflecting on your progress throughout this week helped you set meaningful intentions for your continued healing journey, and what personal commitment will you make to carry this momentum forward?

Journal Prompt: Write your thoughts in your journal.

Conclusion for Chapter 1: Embracing Your Journey

As you conclude this first chapter of your healing journey, take heart in the strength you've discovered within yourself. ***Psalm 46:1-2*** reminds us, ***"God is our refuge and strength, an ever-present help in trouble. Therefore we will not fear, though the earth give way and the mountains fall into the heart of the sea."*** Just as God is our unshakable foundation, you too have begun to build a foundation of resilience, self-awareness, and trust in the process. Each step, no matter how small, has brought you closer to understanding your emotions, embracing vulnerability, and recognizing the power of consistent growth. Healing is not a linear path, but a continuous journey of grace and perseverance.

By reflecting on your journey, celebrating your progress, and setting clear intentions, you have laid the groundwork for continued healing. Trust that, just as God's strength carries you through challenges, your willingness to be vulnerable and open will guide you forward. ***Psalm 46:1-2*** reminds us as well of God's presence in every trial, and as you continue, remember that each step forward is a victory. With God as your refuge, you are building a life filled with faith, resilience, and renewed self-worth, even in the face of difficulties.

Weekly Prayer for the End of Chapter 1: Days 1-7 Embracing Your Journey:

Heavenly Father,

Thank You for guiding me through this first week of my healing journey. I am grateful for Your unwavering presence, and for the strength You have given me to reflect on my emotions, embrace my vulnerabilities, and recognize the progress I've made. As I continue forward, I ask for Your continued guidance and grace to help me remain patient, resilient, and trusting in the process. May Your love remind me that every step I take, no matter how small, is a step toward healing, wholeness, and the life You have planned for me.

In Jesus' name, I pray. Amen.

Chapter 2

Rewriting Your Inner Dialogue

Overcoming Negative Self-Talk and Building Confidence

Days 8-14: Shifting Your Mindset

Chapter 1 of your healing journey focused on recognizing your strengths and laying the foundation for emotional growth and self-worth. Throughout the week, you reflected on your current emotional state and explored how past experiences have shaped your path. You also embraced vulnerability, learning that opening up and being honest with yourself is not a sign of weakness but a source of strength. Each small step forward, whether it was identifying your fears or celebrating your progress, contributed to a greater understanding of yourself and your healing process. This chapter reminded you that healing is not a destination but a journey, requiring patience, trust, and perseverance. *As Psalm 46:1-2* reminds us, ***"God is our refuge and strength, an ever-present help in trouble. Therefore we will not fear."*** You've learned that God's strength is with you, providing refuge as you face your healing process.

As you continued through the exercises, you learned to trust the process, even when results weren't immediately visible. By the end of the chapter, you defined what healing looks like for you personally and set clear intentions for the rest of your journey. The first seven days were about building a foundation—one rooted in self-awareness, emotional resilience, and the belief that every step forward, no matter how small, is a victory. Moving forward, you now have the tools and insights to continue this process with confidence and hope, knowing that God's presence is your strength in every challenge, just as the psalm assures.

In *Chapter 2: Rewriting Your Inner Dialogue— Overcoming Negative Self-Talk and Building Confidence,* we focus on how the words we speak to ourselves have a profound impact on our self-worth and confidence. Negative self-talk can become a powerful barrier to personal growth and healing, often causing us to view ourselves through a lens of doubt, fear, and inadequacy. However, just as the words we speak to others matter, the inner dialogue we engage in must be guided by kindness, truth, and encouragement. *Ephesians 4:29* (NIV) reminds us, ***"Do not let any unwholesome talk come out of your mouths, but only what is helpful for building others up according to their needs, that it may benefit those who listen."*** This scripture is not only about the words we say aloud but also applies to the internal conversations we have with ourselves. Just as we are called to build others up with our words, we must also build ourselves up through positive, life-giving dialogue.

To rewrite your inner dialogue, it's important to first identify the negative thoughts that are holding you back. Often, these thoughts come from past experiences, fears, or external influences, but they do not reflect the truth of who you are. When you catch yourself in a cycle of negative self-talk, pause and ask whether your words are in alignment with the truth of

God's love and grace for you. By shifting your focus from criticism to compassion, you begin to cultivate a mindset that builds your confidence and strengthens your sense of self-worth. Just as *Ephesians 4:29* encourages us to speak what is "helpful for building others up," this is an invitation to speak words of affirmation and encouragement to yourself, replacing harsh judgments with words that nurture your growth.

As you work through this chapter, remember that rewriting your inner dialogue is a process that requires practice and patience. Each time you choose to speak kindly to yourself, you are reinforcing the truth that you are worthy of love, healing, and confidence. Let this be a time to nurture a spirit of self-compassion, where you become your own source of support and encouragement. By overcoming negative self-talk and focusing on building yourself up, you are embracing a powerful tool for personal transformation, allowing your inner voice to reflect the truth of your inherent value and potential. Through this practice, you will grow in confidence and build a strong foundation for future growth.

Weekly Prayer for Chapter 2: Rewriting Your Inner Dialogue

Heavenly Father,

I come before You with humble hearts as I begin Chapter 2 of this journey. I thank You for the strength You have provided thus far and for the progress made in recognizing the power of our inner dialogue. As I focus on rewriting the negative self-talk that has held me back, I ask for Your guidance in transforming these thoughts into words of life. Help me to see ourselves through Your eyes—worthy, loved, and capable of growth. Lord, give me the wisdom to embrace this process with patience and perseverance, trusting that each step forward is a reflection of Your grace working within me.

Lord, as I work on shifting my mindset, may Your Word be the foundation of my confidence. Let Your truth replace every lie and doubt that seeks to diminish my worth. I stand on Your promise *in Ephesians 4:29*, that I will speak only what is helpful for building up, not only to others but to myself. Bless this chapter and the transformation it will bring.

In Jesus' name, I pray, Amen.

Workbook Lessons Week 2

Rewriting Your Inner Dialogue

Overcoming Negative Self-Talk and Building Confidence

Overcoming negative self-talk is a crucial step toward building lasting confidence and shifting your mindset to one of growth and self-empowerment. Negative self-talk often stems from past experiences, doubts, and fears, shaping how we perceive ourselves and our abilities. These internal dialogues can become habitual, silently undermining our self-esteem and limiting our potential. However, by becoming aware of these harmful thought patterns, we can begin to rewrite the narrative in our minds. Replacing negative thoughts with positive affirmations and truths is essential in building confidence. This process involves consciously choosing to speak words of kindness, compassion, and encouragement to yourself, fostering a mindset that empowers rather than diminishes you.

Shifting your mindset requires a consistent commitment to viewing challenges as opportunities for growth rather than as confirmation of inadequacy. By embracing a growth mindset, you begin to see failure and setbacks not as personal failures, but as steppingstones toward personal development and success. Confidence is built when you believe in your ability to learn, grow, and improve over time. Each time you intentionally choose to silence negative self-talk and replace it with empowering thoughts, you are reshaping your mind to align with the truth of your value and potential. Over time, this shift will lead to greater self-assurance, resilience, and a deep-seated belief that you are capable of achieving your goals.

Workbook Lesson: Day 8 - Identifying Negative Self-Talk

Shifting Your Mindset

Identifying negative self-talk is a crucial step in shifting your mindset toward healing and growth. Often, the thoughts we repeat to ourselves are the most harmful, yet we may not even realize they're happening. Negative self-talk can manifest in subtle ways, such as doubting your abilities, criticizing your appearance, or blaming yourself for things beyond your control. These thoughts create mental barriers, holding you back from embracing your true potential and confidence. To shift your mindset, it's important to bring awareness to these negative thoughts, recognize their patterns, and understand how they've influenced your beliefs about yourself.

Once you've identified your negative self-talk, the next step is to reframe these thoughts in a way that promotes positivity and growth. This doesn't mean ignoring or suppressing negative emotions but rather transforming harmful narratives into constructive affirmations. By consistently replacing negative thoughts with empowering ones, you gradually reshape your mindset, allowing room for self-compassion, confidence, and resilience. The process takes practice, but with time, you'll find that shifting your inner dialogue leads to a stronger, more positive relationship with yourself.

Purpose:

The purpose of this exercise is to help you recognize the common negative thoughts that run through your mind, often holding you back from achieving your full potential.

Introduction:

Negative self-talk can be subtle but powerful, shaping how you see yourself and the world. It might show up in moments of doubt, self-criticism, or fear. Today's lesson will guide you to identify these recurring thoughts so you can begin the process of shifting them.

Reflection Exercise:

1. **Identify Common Negative Thoughts:** Identifying common negative thoughts, like "I'm not good enough" or "I'll never succeed," is the first step in transforming your mindset. Recognizing these patterns lets you challenge and replace them with positive beliefs that align with your true worth and potential.

   Journal Prompt: Write down 3-5 negative thoughts that regularly appear in your mind. It could be doubts about your abilities, your worth, or your future.

   _____

   _____

   _____

2. **Consider the Source:** Understanding the source of your negative thoughts helps reveal whether they stem from past experiences, criticism, or societal pressures. By pinpointing these origins, you can separate yourself from limiting beliefs and embrace a more positive self-view.

Journal Prompt: Reflect on where these thoughts may have originated. Are they tied to past experiences, words others have said, or fears of the unknown?

_____

_____

_____

3. **Reframe Your Negative Thoughts:** Once you've identified your negative thoughts, take a moment to challenge them. Ask yourself if there's evidence supporting these thoughts or if they're assumptions you've made. Then, try to reframe each negative thought with a positive, empowering alternative that's more in line with your values and goals.

Journal Prompt: Write down one of your common negative thoughts and then reframe it with a positive statement. For example, if you often think, "I always fail," reframe it as, "Every setback is a learning opportunity for growth." Describe how this new perspective feels and how it can positively impact your mindset.

_____

_____

_____

Reflection Question:

How does recognizing your negative self-talk make you more aware of the areas where you need to grow?

> *Journal Prompt:* In your journal, describe a recent moment when you noticed negative self-talk. Write about how this awareness highlighted areas where you'd like to grow, and list one or two small actions you can take to start changing these thought.

_____

_____

_____

Day 8 – Conclusion: Breaking Free: Shifting from Negative Self-Talk to Empowerment

In conclusion, Day 8 has brought you one step closer to transforming the way you perceive yourself by addressing the negative self-talk that may have quietly shaped your thoughts for years. By identifying these patterns, you've opened the door to a new level of awareness, giving yourself the opportunity to shift your mindset from one of self-doubt to self-empowerment. The process of recognizing and reframing these harmful thoughts is not an overnight change, but each step you take today is a crucial part of building a healthier and more resilient inner dialogue.

As you continue to work through these lessons, remember that transforming negative self-talk is a practice that requires patience and self-compassion. Every time you challenge a negative thought, you're actively choosing to rewrite your narrative. With time, this consistent effort will allow you to develop a mindset grounded in self-worth, confidence, and positivity, ultimately leading to deeper healing and personal growth. Keep moving forward—one thought at a time, you're reclaiming your power.

Workbook Lesson: Day 9 - Reframing Negative Thoughts Purpose

Turning Doubts into Opportunities for Growth

Doubts often act as barriers to personal growth, making us feel stuck and unsure of our path. However, these moments of uncertainty can be transformed into powerful opportunities for growth when we choose to view them through a new lens. Instead of allowing doubts to cripple our confidence, we can see them as an invitation to deepen our faith and strengthen our resolve. By leaning into the process of growth, we can begin to see our doubts as steppingstones that lead us to greater clarity and purpose. Just as the Bible reminds us in *James 1:3-4*

(NIV): *"Because you know that the testing of your faith produces perseverance. Let perseverance finish its work so that you may be mature and complete, not lacking anything."* This scripture encourages us to embrace the challenges that come with doubt, trusting that they serve a greater purpose in shaping our strength and resilience.

When we shift our perspective on doubt, it opens the door to new possibilities. Rather than fearing uncertainty, we can approach it with curiosity and faith, asking God to reveal the lessons hidden within our doubts. This process of reframing doubt allows us to grow in wisdom and spiritual maturity, transforming what once held us back into a catalyst for progress. As we rely on God's guidance through these moments, we can take heart in knowing that our doubts are not the end of the story but the beginning of a deeper journey of faith. In *Proverbs 3:5-6* (NIV), we are reminded: *"Trust in the Lord with all your heart and lean not on your own understanding; in all your ways submit to him, and he will make your paths straight."* This scripture assures us that when we surrender our doubts to God, He will direct our steps and turn our uncertainty into growth.

Purpose

The purpose of reframing negative thoughts is to transform harmful, limiting beliefs into empowering and constructive ones. By shifting your mindset, you allow yourself to break free from patterns of self-doubt and criticism that hold you back. Reframing is not about dismissing or ignoring your challenges but learning to view them from a more compassionate and growth-oriented perspective. This process helps you build resilience, improve self-worth, and foster a healthier, more positive inner dialogue, which ultimately supports your emotional healing and personal development.

The purpose of today's exercise is to learn how to take the negative thoughts you identified and reframe them into positive, empowering affirmations.

Introduction:

Reframing is a powerful tool that helps you take control of your internal dialogue. Instead of accepting negative thoughts as facts, you'll learn how to reframe them in a way that affirms your worth and potential. Today, we will practice turning those harmful thoughts into affirmations that build you up.

Reflection Exercise:

1. **Reframe the Thought:** Take the negative thoughts you wrote down yesterday and write a positive, truth-based affirmation to counter each one. For example, if your thought was, "I'm not good enough," reframe it to, "I am capable and worthy of success."

   Journal Prompt: Write a positive, truth-based affirmation

   _____

   _____

   _____

2. **Practice Reframing:** Throughout the day, whenever a negative thought arises, consciously practice reframing it into an empowering statement.

   Journal Prompt: Throughout the day, notice any negative thoughts that arise and write them down. Then, take a moment to reframe each one into a positive, empowering statement. At the end of the day, review and write your list, reflect on how reframing your thoughts made you feel.

   _____

   _____

   _____

3. **Embrace the Lessons in Doubt:** Reflect on a recent moment of doubt and consider what it might be teaching you about yourself or your path. Instead of viewing doubt as a setback, think of it as an opportunity for growth and discovery. What strengths or new perspectives might emerge from this experience?

Journal Prompt: Write down a recent moment of doubt and explore any lessons or insights it offered. How can you use this experience to reinforce your faith, deepen your self-understanding, and build resilience on your journey?

_____

_____

_____

Reflection Question:

How does reframing negative thoughts help you see yourself in a more positive and compassionate way?

Journal Prompt: Write down a negative thought you've recently experienced and then reframe it into a more positive and compassionate perspective. Reflect on how this shift makes you feel about yourself and how it encourages you to view yourself with kindness and understanding.

_____

_____

_____

Day 9 – Conclusion: Embracing Growth Through Reframing Negative Thoughts

As we conclude Chapter 9 on reframing negative thoughts, we are reminded that doubt and negative self-talk, while challenging, can serve as powerful opportunities for growth. By choosing to reframe these thoughts, we transform limiting beliefs into empowering affirmations that align with our true potential. This process, though gradual, helps break the cycle of self-doubt and fosters a more compassionate and growth-oriented perspective. As *James 1:3-4* reminds us, the testing of our faith produces perseverance, and this perseverance leads to maturity and strength. By leaning into this journey with faith and intentionality, we not only reshape our inner dialogue but also open the door to greater resilience, healing, and self-worth. Trust that each reframed thought is a step toward a more empowered and fulfilling life, grounded in God's wisdom and grace.

Workbook Lesson: Day 10 - Speaking Kindly to Yourself

Cultivating Self-Compassion: The Power of Speaking Kindly to Yourself

Speaking kindly to yourself is essential for building self-worth and fostering emotional healing. Often, we are our own harshest critics, holding ourselves to impossible standards and engaging in negative self-talk that reinforces feelings of inadequacy. Day 10 focuses on shifting this narrative by cultivating a habit of self-compassionate language. In *Ephesians 4:29* (NIV), we are reminded, ***"Do not let any unwholesome talk come out of your mouths, but only what is helpful for building others up according to their needs."*** This verse also applies to the way we speak to ourselves. Speaking kindly to yourself means giving yourself the grace to make mistakes, recognizing your strengths, and embracing your humanity. By replacing negative thoughts with gentle, encouraging words, you begin to create a more nurturing inner dialogue that supports your growth and well-being.

This practice of self-kindness doesn't mean avoiding accountability or ignoring areas for improvement. Instead, it's about approaching your journey with understanding and patience. Just as you would offer a friend compassion during their struggles, you deserve to give yourself the same care. As you develop the habit of speaking kindly to yourself, you'll notice a shift in how you view challenges, setbacks, and even successes. You'll start to see yourself as worthy of love and respect, which will help you build a solid foundation for long-lasting confidence and inner peace.

Purpose:

Today's focus is on developing the habit of speaking kindly to yourself and incorporating self-compassion into your daily thoughts.

Introduction:

Self-compassion is crucial for building confidence and healing. Just as you would speak kindly to a friend going through a tough time, you must learn to treat yourself with the same kindness and understanding. Today, we will focus on developing a kinder, more compassionate inner dialogue.

Reflection Exercise:

1. **Notice Your Language:** Throughout the day, notice how you speak to yourself, especially in challenging moments. Are your words compassionate or critical?

   Journal Prompt: Write down a few examples of how you spoke to yourself today, especially during challenging moments. Were your words compassionate or critical? Reflect on how your inner dialogue made you feel and consider why these specific thoughts came up.

_____

_____

_____

2. **Rewrite the Script:** Whenever you catch yourself being harsh or judgmental, stop and replace those words with something kinder and more supportive.

   Journal Prompt: Throughout the day, record any moments where you noticed yourself speaking harshly or judgmentally. Take a moment to rewrite each of these negative statements with kinder, more supportive words. How did this shift in language impact your mood and perspective on the situation?

   _____

   _____

   _____

3: **Embrace Your Progress:** Reflect on a recent challenge or setback and consider how you responded to yourself during that time. Did you encourage yourself with kindness, or did you focus on criticism? Take a moment to acknowledge the progress you've made, no matter how small, and practice offering yourself words of affirmation that celebrate this progress.

> *Journal Prompt:* Write down a recent experience where you faced a challenge or felt discouraged. Reflect on how you spoke to yourself in that moment and consider how you can replace any negative self-talk with compassionate and encouraging words. What kind words can you offer yourself to acknowledge your growth and effort?

_____

_____

_____

Reflection Question:

How does changing the way you speak to yourself impact your emotional well-being?

> *Journal Prompt:* Write down how you currently speak to yourself in challenging moments, and then imagine replacing those words with more compassionate and encouraging ones. Reflect on how this shift in language could impact your emotional well-being. How might speaking kindly to yourself change the way you feel about yourself and your ability to handle difficult situations?

_____

_____

_____

Day 10 – Conclusion: Transforming Your Inner Dialogue: The Power of Kindness

As you conclude Chapter 10 on speaking kindly to yourself, you have taken an important step in transforming your inner dialogue. Cultivating self-compassion requires intention, patience, and a willingness to shift from self-criticism to self-care. By recognizing the impact of your words and embracing the practice of speaking kindly to yourself, you lay the foundation for emotional healing and lasting confidence. Remember, just as *Ephesians 4:29* encourages us to build others up with our words, we must also build ourselves up with kindness and understanding. As you continue to rewrite the narrative within, you will experience greater self-worth and inner peace, enabling you to navigate your journey with grace and resilience.

Workbook Lesson: Day 11 - Affirmations for Healing

Harnessing the Power of Affirmations for Healing

Affirmations for healing are transformative tools that not only shift our mindset but also align our thoughts with God's truth about who we are. As **Proverbs 18:21** (NIV) reminds us, **"The tongue has the power of life and death,"** emphasizing the profound impact of the words we speak over ourselves. By intentionally creating affirmations that reflect God's promises, we replace negative self-talk with declarations rooted in faith. These affirmations—such as **"I am fearfully and wonderfully made"** (**Psalm 139:14**)—help reinforce our identity in Christ, fostering a mindset of self-compassion, confidence, and emotional healing. Speaking these life-giving truths invites God's healing power into our hearts and minds, enabling us to break free from limiting beliefs and embrace the fullness of His love and purpose.

As you create personal affirmations on Day 11, remember that they are more than just positive statements—they are declarations of God's promises over your life. Each time you speak these affirmations, you are actively choosing to align your thoughts with His Word, allowing His truth to replace the lies of doubt, fear, and inadequacy. Whether you are affirming your worth, strength, or resilience, these declarations have the power to renew your mind and transform your journey of healing. By consistently practicing these affirmations, you will cultivate a deeper sense of self-worth and confidence, knowing that your identity is firmly rooted in God's love and grace.

Purpose:
Today's exercise will help you create a set of personal affirmations that you can use daily to reinforce positive thinking and healing.

Introduction:
Affirmations are positive, truth-based statements that can help you overcome self-doubt, fear, and negativity. By speaking these affirmations daily, you begin to reshape your mindset and

align your thoughts with the truth of who you are. Today, you'll create your own set of affirmations for healing and growth.

Reflection Exercise:

1. **Create Your Affirmations:** Take a few moments to transform any negative thoughts into positive, empowering statements that uplift you. Choose words that reflect your worth, potential, and resilience, and repeat them daily to reinforce a compassionate, supportive inner dialogue.

    Journal Prompt: Write 5-7 personal affirmations that reflect the kind of healing and growth you want to experience. These should be statements you can say to yourself every day, such as "I am worthy of love and respect" or "I am growing stronger each day."

---

2. **Daily Practice:** Commit to saying these affirmations out loud each morning or before bed, letting them sink into your heart and mind.

3. **Reflect on Impact**: After practicing your affirmations for a week, take a moment to reflect on any changes you've noticed in your thoughts, emotions, or behavior.

   Journal Prompt: Write about how speaking your affirmations daily has influenced your self-perception and emotional well-being. What positive shifts have you experienced, and how do these affirmations continue to empower you on your healing journey?

   _____

   _____

   _____

Reflection Question:

How do daily affirmations help you stay focused on your healing and personal growth?

Journal Prompt: Write about specific ways they help you stay focused on your healing and personal growth, including any moments where affirmations have inspired you to take positive actions or overcome challenges.

_____

_____

_____

Day 11 – Conclusion: Embracing God's Truth: The Power of Daily Affirmations

As you conclude Day 11, remember that the affirmations you've created are not just positive words—they are powerful declarations of God's truth over your life. Each time you speak these affirmations, you are actively reshaping your mindset, aligning your thoughts with His promises, and inviting His healing presence into your heart. The process of consistently speaking life-giving words will help you break free from negative self-talk and foster a deeper sense of self-worth and confidence. By embracing these daily affirmations, you are reinforcing your identity in Christ, allowing His truth to guide you toward continued healing, growth, and a stronger, more resilient mindset. Keep nurturing this practice, knowing that each affirmation brings you closer to fully embracing the person God has called you to be.

Workbook Lesson: Day 12 - Letting Go of Past Labels

Releasing the Weight of Past Labels

Letting go of the label's others have placed on you is a transformative step in your healing journey. These labels, whether spoken by others or formed from past experiences, often shape the way you see yourself and hinder your ability to fully embrace the freedom God has designed for your life. They can feel like heavy burdens, holding you back from stepping into your true identity. However, in *2 Corinthians 5:17*, we are reminded that, in Christ, we are a new creation: *"The old has gone, the new is here!"* This powerful truth assures us that our past does not define us; we are no longer bound by the words and judgments that once limited us. God's love frees us from these labels, offering us a fresh identity grounded in His grace and love.

As you move forward, it's important to release the labels that have influenced your self-image and embrace the truth of who God says you are. Instead of allowing words like "unworthy" or "broken" to shape your confidence, begin to replace them with the truth that you are beloved, chosen, and redeemed. *Ephesians 1:4* reminds us that God chose you long before the world was created, and in His sight, you are holy and blameless. By letting go of the labels of the past, you free yourself to walk confidently in the identity God has given you. This new identity not only brings healing but also empowers you to live boldly and purposefully, knowing that you are defined by God's love and not by the opinions of others.

Purpose:

The purpose of this lesson is to release the labels others have placed on you that don't define your worth.

Introduction:

Sometimes, the labels others have placed on you—such as "not smart enough," "too sensitive," or "unworthy"—can become ingrained in your identity. Today's exercise will help you let go of these limiting labels and redefine yourself based on your truth.

Reflection Exercise:

1. **List the Labels: List the Labels:** Take a moment to reflect on the labels or judgments you've internalized from others, whether they stem from past experiences or current interactions.

Journal Prompt: Write down any labels or judgments you have accepted from others that don't align with your true worth.

_____

_____

_____

2. **Release the Labels:** Mentally and emotionally release these labels, affirming that they do not define you.

   Journal Prompt: Write down who you truly are in place of these labels.

_____

_____

_____

3. **Embrace Your True Identity:** Reflect on the qualities and strengths that truly define you, beyond the labels that have been imposed upon you. Journal Prompt: Write down positive affirmations that highlight your true

identity, focusing on the aspects of yourself that you cherish and that align with God's truth about who you are.

Journal Prompt: Write down a time when you felt liberated from a label that no longer served you. What specific steps did you take to let go of that label, and how did embracing your true identity impact your self-perception and confidence? Write about the emotions you experienced during this process and how it has shaped your journey moving forward.

Reflection Question:

What labels have you allowed to define you, and how can letting go of them set you free?

Journal Prompt: Write a time when you felt liberated from a label that no longer served you. What specific steps did you take to let go of that label, and how did embracing your true identity impact your self-perception and confidence? Write about the emotions you experienced during this process and how it has shaped your journey moving forward.

_____

_____

_____

Day 12 – Conclusion: Releasing Past Labels: Embracing Your True Identity in Christ

Letting go of the past labels that others have placed on you is a significant step toward reclaiming your true identity in Christ. As you release these limiting labels, you free yourself from the burdens of false perceptions and judgments, allowing God's truth to shape how you see yourself. In *2 Corinthians 5:17*, we are reminded that through Christ, we are made new, and the old labels no longer have power over us. By embracing this truth and affirming your worth in God's eyes, you begin to see yourself as beloved, chosen, and redeemed. As you continue your healing journey, remember that your identity is not defined by the words of others but by God's love and purpose for you. Moving forward, let this new understanding empower you to live with confidence and freedom, fully aligned with the truth of who you are in Christ.

Workbook Lesson: Day 13 - Challenging Your Inner Critic

Silencing the Inner Critic: Embracing God's Truth

Challenging your inner critic is essential to breaking free from self-doubt, fear, and shame that can cloud your perception of who you are in God's eyes. This inner critic often whispers lies that amplify feelings of inadequacy and unworthiness, preventing you from embracing the fullness of life that God intends. However, *2 Timothy 1:7* (NIV) reassures us, ***"For the Spirit God gave us does not make us timid, but gives us power, love, and self-discipline."*** This verse reminds us that we have the power through God's Spirit to confront and silence these negative voices, reclaiming our confidence and sense of worth. By challenging the lies of the inner critic, you open the door to living a life grounded in love, strength, and self-discipline.

As you continue this process, remember that your worth is rooted in God's love, not in the critical thoughts that arise in moments of fear or doubt. *Romans 12:2* (NIV) instructs us *to* ***"be transformed by the renewing of your mind,"*** emphasizing the importance of replacing negative thoughts with affirmations of God's truth. You are fearfully and wonderfully made, beloved, and redeemed—no criticism can diminish this truth. By embracing God's promises and silencing the inner critic, you cultivate a mindset of peace, confidence, and self-compassion, allowing you to walk forward in faith and live fully in your true identity.

Purpose:

Today's exercise is about confronting and challenging your

inner critic, the voice that tells you that you're not good enough or worthy.

Introduction:

Your inner critic can be harsh and relentless, but it's important to realize that it doesn't speak the truth. Challenging this voice requires courage and the understanding that you are worthy of kindness, respect, and love. Today, we will focus on quieting your inner critic and replacing its voice with one of compassion.

Reflection Exercise:

1. **Confront Your Inner Critic:** Identify the most common criticisms your inner critic tells you.

   Journal Prompt: When you listen to your inner critic, what are the common criticisms you hear?

   _____

   _____

   _____

2. **Challenge Its Lies:** For each criticism, challenge its validity and replace it with a compassionate and affirming statement. For example, if your inner critic says, "You're a failure," challenge that by affirming, "I am learning and growing with each experience."

   Journal Prompt: Write down each criticism and replace it with a compassionate and affirming statement.

   _____

   _____

   _____

3. **Visualize Your True Self:** Take a moment to envision yourself without the influence of your inner critic. Picture how you would feel, act, and perceive your worth if you fully embraced God's truth about who you are.

   Journal Prompt: Write about the qualities and strengths that shine through when you silence your inner critic. How would your life change if you operated from a place of self-love and acceptance instead of self-judgment?

Reflect on the emotions and confidence you would gain from embracing this version of yourself.

_____

_____

_____

Reflection Question:

How does challenging your inner critic change the way you perceive yourself and your abilities?

Journal Prompt: Write a specific instance where you challenged your inner critic. How did this shift in perspective influence your view of yourself and your capabilities? Write about any positive changes you noticed in your self-perception and confidence, and how this newfound understanding can empower you in future situations.

_____

_____

_____

Day 13 – Conclusion: Overcoming the Inner Critic: Embracing Your God-Given Identity

In conclusion, silencing your inner critic is a vital step toward embracing the truth of your identity in Christ. The inner critic's negative voice often stems from fear, doubt, and past experiences, yet it does not define your worth or your potential. As *2 Timothy 1:7* reminds us, God has given you a spirit of power, love, and self-discipline, equipping you with the strength to confront and challenge those critical thoughts. By consistently replacing the lies of the inner critic with affirmations rooted in God's promises, such as ***Romans 12:2***, you are renewing your mind and aligning your thoughts with His truth. As you continue this process, you will cultivate a mindset filled with confidence, peace, and self-compassion, allowing you to live boldly in the fullness of who God created you to be.

Workbook Lesson: Day 14 - Building Confidence through Affirmation

Strengthening Confidence through Daily Affirmations

Affirmations are powerful tools that reshape how we view ourselves and the world around us, serving as intentional, positive statements that realign our mindset with truth. When we speak affirmations rooted in truth, we counter negative self-talk and replace doubt with self-assurance. This practice helps to remind us of our worth, capabilities, and potential, gradually shifting our mindset from insecurity to confidence. By repeating affirmations consistently, we nurture a sense of courage and resilience, empowering ourselves to face life's challenges with grace. Affirming who we are and what we are capable of each day builds a strong foundation for personal growth and emotional well-being.

More than just building confidence in ourselves, affirmations also align our hearts with God's truth. **Proverbs 18:21** reminds us that ***"the tongue has the power of life and death,"*** emphasizing how the words we speak to ourselves can either uplift or hinder our spirit. When we choose to declare affirmations grounded in God's promises, we begin to see ourselves as He sees us—fearfully and wonderfully made, equipped for growth, and deeply loved. By practicing daily affirmations, we not only boost our self-confidence but also strengthen our identity in Christ, knowing that we are worthy of love, success, and the fullness of life He has designed for us.

Purpose:
Today's focus is on reflecting on how daily affirmations and kind words have begun to shift your mindset and build your confidence.

Introduction:
Affirmations and kind words have a profound impact on your self-perception. By consistently speaking truth and compassion into your life, you are building a solid foundation of confidence. Today, you will reflect on the changes you've

noticed in yourself after practicing positive affirmations and self-compassion.

Reflection Exercise:

1. **Reflect on Your Growth:** Reflecting on your growth allows you to recognize the progress you've made, even in small steps, which reinforces your journey toward healing and self-acceptance. Acknowledging these milestones empowers you to embrace future challenges with confidence and resilience.

   Journal Prompt: Write down any shifts in your mindset or self-confidence that you've noticed since you began practicing affirmations and kind words. How have these practices helped you see yourself in a more positive light?

   _____

   _____

   _____

2. **Set a New Intention:** Based on the growth you've experienced, set an intention for how you will continue to use affirmations and positive language moving forward.

Journal Prompt: Write down a specific intention for incorporating affirmations and positive language into your daily routine. How will you remind yourself to speak kindly to yourself, and what steps will you take to ensure this positive mindset continues to support your growth and healing journey?

_____

_____

_____

3. **Celebrate Your Progress:** Recognizing and celebrating your achievements, no matter how small, is crucial for building lasting confidence. Reflect on the specific moments when you've successfully used affirmations and

how these instances have positively influenced your self-image and actions.

Journal Prompt: Write about a recent experience where you consciously used affirmations to boost your confidence. How did it make you feel, and what positive changes did you notice in your behavior or mindset as a result? Consider how celebrating these moments can reinforce your commitment to using affirmations in the future.

_____

_____

_____

Reflection Question:

How have daily affirmations and positive self-talk contributed to your growing confidence, and how can you continue to strengthen this practice in your daily life?

Journal Prompt: Write specific instances where daily affirmations and positive self-talk have helped you feel more confident. How have these practices influenced your thoughts and actions, and what strategies can you implement to ensure you consistently incorporate affirmations into your daily routine for ongoing growth and empowerment?

_____

_____

_____

Day 14 – Conclusion: Empowered by Words: Harnessing the Strength of Affirmations

The power of affirmations lies in their ability to reshape our mindset, transforming doubt into confidence and negativity into self-compassion. As you've journeyed through Day 14, you've experienced firsthand how consistently speaking positive affirmations and kind words into your life builds a foundation of confidence and emotional well-being. Affirmations, especially those rooted in God's truth, have allowed you to realign your thoughts with your worth and potential, nurturing resilience and courage. ***Proverbs 18:21*** reminds us that our words have power, and through this practice, you have begun to see yourself as God sees you—capable, loved, and deeply valued. Moving forward, continue to harness the strength of affirmations to reinforce your growing confidence, knowing that each affirmation builds a stronger, more empowered version of yourself.

Activity:

"Breaking Free: Rewriting Your Inner Script"

Objective:

This activity is designed to help you break free from negative self-talk and create a new, empowering internal narrative. By identifying and challenging limiting beliefs, you will develop positive affirmations that align with your true value and identity.

Instructions:

Step 1: Creating Your "Old Story"

- Take 10 minutes to reflect on the negative self-talk or limiting beliefs that frequently arise in your mind.

- *Journal Prompt:* Write down 3-5 common negative statements that you say to yourself. Examples could include: "I'm not good enough," "I always fail," or "I don't deserve success."

_____

_____

_____

Step 2: Rewriting the Narrative

- Now, transform each negative statement into a positive, empowering affirmation. For example, change "I'm not good enough" to "I am capable and worthy of success."

- *Journal Prompt:* Write down each new affirmation next to its corresponding negative thought.

Step 3: Visualization Exercise

- Close your eyes and imagine a scene where you are fully embodying these new affirmations. Visualize yourself confidently walking into a situation where you would normally feel doubt or fear.

- See yourself succeeding, feeling empowered, and speaking kindly to yourself throughout the process. Hold this vision for 5 minutes, repeating your affirmations silently.

Step 4: Daily Affirmation Ritual

- Commit to saying this affirmation out loud at least three times a day, especially during moments when negative self-talk would typically emerge

- *Journal Prompt:* Choose one of your new affirmations to focus on for the next 7 days. Write it on a sticky note and place it somewhere you'll see it often, like your mirror or desk.

_____

_____

_____

Step 5: Reflection

- After practicing your affirmation for one week, reflect on any changes in your mindset or emotional state. How has your new narrative impacted the way you view yourself?

- *Journal Prompt:* Write down your thoughts in your journal, noting any shifts in confidence, self-compassion, or motivation.

_____

_____

_____

Bonus Step: Affirmation Art

- For a creative twist, take some time to visually represent your new affirmations. Using markers, paint, or digital tools, create an "Affirmation Board" filled with positive statements, images, and colors that inspire you. Place it somewhere you can see it daily for ongoing motivation.

Reflection Question: How has rewriting your internal dialogue affected your confidence and outlook?

> ***Journal Prompt:*** Write down how can you continue to integrate positive affirmations into your daily routine to reinforce a mindset of growth and empowerment?

---   ---------

Conclusion for Chapter 2: Rewriting Your Inner Dialogue

In Chapter 2, you embarked on the challenging yet rewarding journey of confronting and transforming your inner dialogue. Throughout the week, you explored the impact of negative self-talk and began the process of rewriting those harmful narratives. By identifying limiting beliefs, reframing negative thoughts, and practicing self-compassion, you have taken significant steps toward building a mindset that nurtures your growth. As *Ephesians 4:29* reminds us, ***"Do not let any unwholesome talk come out of your mouths, but only what is helpful for building others up."*** This scripture not only applies to how we speak to others but also reflects the importance of speaking kindly to ourselves. Each time you replace a negative thought with a positive affirmation, you are strengthening your self-worth and confidence.

The lessons in this chapter have equipped you with tools to challenge your inner critic, let go of past labels, and build lasting confidence through affirmation. You've learned that true transformation comes not from perfection but from consistent, intentional steps forward. Rewriting your inner dialogue is an ongoing process, one that requires patience and practice. However, by continuing to speak words of kindness and truth into your life, you are reinforcing the belief that you are worthy of love, success, and healing. As you move forward, embrace these practices with the knowledge that every positive thought and affirmation is a building block in your journey toward self-empowerment and confidence.

As you continue to rewrite your inner dialogue, remember that transformation doesn't happen overnight. It's a gradual process, but each time you choose self-compassion over self-criticism, you are reshaping your mindset and laying the foundation for long-term growth. The negative thoughts that once held you back are losing their power as you cultivate a narrative that aligns with your true value. By speaking affirmations rooted in kindness and truth, you're creating a space for healing and confidence to flourish. Moving forward, let this chapter be a reminder that your words have power—not only in how you engage with others but in how you speak to and affirm yourself.

Weekly Prayer for end of Chapter 2: Rewriting Your Inner Dialogue

Heavenly Father,

Thank You for guiding me through this journey of rewriting my inner dialogue and overcoming negative self-talk. As I learn to speak words of kindness, truth, and affirmation to myself, I ask for Your strength to silence the inner critic and embrace the confidence You have placed within me. Help me to see myself as You see me—worthy, loved, and capable of great things. May Your Word continue to renew my mind and guide me toward a mindset of growth, healing, and self-compassion.

In Jesus' name, I pray. Amen.

Chapter 3:

Building Resilience Through Self-Worth

Strengthening Your Foundation for Lasting Change

Days 15-21: Creating a Resilient Mindset

In Chapter 2, *Rewriting Your Inner Dialogue: Overcoming Negative Self-Talk and Building Confidence*, you embarked on a transformative journey of shifting your mindset and learning to speak kindly to yourself. Throughout Days 8-14, you focused on identifying the negative self-talk that often holds you back, reframing these harmful thoughts, and developing self-compassionate language. By doing this, you began to see how powerful your inner dialogue can be in shaping your confidence and self-worth. As you practiced daily affirmations and challenged the limiting beliefs that have defined you for so long, you started to rebuild your sense of self, aligning your thoughts with truth and positivity. ***Ephesians 4:29*** reminds us, ***"Do not let any unwholesome talk come out of your mouths, but only what is helpful for building others up,"*** and this includes how we speak to ourselves.

This chapter also guided you in letting go of past labels and silencing your inner critic. By embracing a mindset of growth, you recognized that setbacks and challenges are not reflections of your worth, but rather opportunities for learning and personal development. Through this process, you have begun to rewrite your internal narrative, replacing harsh judgments with life-giving affirmations that nurture your growth. As you move forward, continue to reinforce these positive changes by practicing affirmations, speaking kindly to yourself, and trusting in the power of your renewed mindset to build lasting confidence and resilience. Let ***Ephesians 4:29*** continue to remind you of the importance of speaking what builds you up, allowing your words to reflect the truth of who you are.

Resilience is the ability to withstand adversity, overcome obstacles, and grow stronger in the face of challenges. In this chapter, we focus on building a resilient mindset that is rooted in self-worth and faith. True resilience doesn't mean avoiding hardship, but rather confronting it with confidence and trust in God's strength. ***Philippians 4:13*** reminds us, ***"I can do all this through Him who gives me strength."*** This powerful truth highlights the source of our resilience—God's strength within us. By embracing our self-worth and relying on His power, we develop the resilience needed to navigate life's difficulties and create lasting change.

Developing a resilient mindset starts with understanding your value in Christ. Your self-worth is not based on external achievements, approval from others, or even your past mistakes. Instead, it is grounded in the unwavering love and purpose God has for you. When you recognize your inherent worth, you become less shaken by setbacks or criticism, because your foundation is secure. This sense of self-worth gives you the confidence to face challenges head-on, knowing that no matter what happens, you are still deeply loved and valued by God.

Resilience also involves reframing how we see difficulties. Rather than viewing obstacles as threats, we can see them as opportunities for growth. When we shift our perspective, we realize that every challenge is a chance to deepen our faith, develop our character, and grow stronger in our sense of self-worth. *Philippians 4:13* encourages us to remember that, through God's strength, we can endure and thrive, no matter the circumstances. Each step you take to create a resilient mindset is a step toward becoming the person God has called you to be, someone who stands firm in the face of adversity.

Finally, building resilience through self-worth is an ongoing process. It requires patience, persistence, and faith in God's plan. There will be moments when you feel weak or unsure, but it is in these times that you can lean on the promise of *Philippians 4:13* and trust that God's strength will carry you through. By nurturing a resilient mindset, you are not only preparing yourself to handle life's challenges but also creating a strong foundation for lasting change. With every step forward, you are building the emotional, mental, and spiritual strength needed to live a life of purpose, confidence, and resilience.

Weekly Prayer for Chapter 3: Building Resilience Through Self-Worth

Heavenly Father,

As I begin Chapter 3 of this journey, I come before You with open hearts, seeking Your strength and guidance. Thank You for the progress made in transforming my inner dialogue and learning to speak kindly to myself. Now, as I focus on building resilience through self-worth, I ask for Your wisdom and grace to help me see myself as You see me—fearfully and wonderfully made, strong in Your love. Remind me, Lord, that true resilience comes from trusting in Your strength, and with You, I can face any challenge. Strengthen our hearts and minds as I continue this journey, and help me to stand firm in my self-worth, knowing that through You, I can overcome every obstacle.

I also thank You, God, for guiding me through the first two chapters of this journey. Thank You for teaching me to recognize my strengths, embrace vulnerability, and silence the negative voices that once held me back. I am grateful for the growth and transformation You have already brought into my life. May the foundation of self-worth and confidence that You have helped me build continue to grow stronger as I move forward. I trust in Your presence every step of the way, knowing that Your love is the source of my resilience.

In Jesus' name, I pray. Amen.

Workbook Lessons Week 3

Building Resilience Through Self-Worth

Strengthening Your Foundation for Lasting Change

In week 3, you will focus on cultivating a resilient mindset by strengthening your foundation of self-worth. Resilience, the ability to bounce back from challenges and adversity, is deeply connected to how you perceive and value yourself. When you understand your inherent worth, you develop the emotional and mental strength needed to overcome life's difficulties with confidence and grace. Throughout the next seven days, we will explore key concepts such as defining self-worth, setting healthy boundaries, practicing self-compassion, and developing emotional resilience. Each lesson is designed to help you anchor your confidence in the truth of your value, allowing you to navigate challenges with a steady, resilient mindset.

As you move through this week, you will begin to see how your self-worth influences every aspect of your life, from your relationships to the way you handle setbacks. By embracing your worth, you will discover the power of self-forgiveness, the strength in setting boundaries, and the courage to cultivate mental and emotional resilience. This chapter invites you to see yourself through a new lens—one that honors your value and empowers you to face challenges with unwavering belief in your ability to grow and succeed. Welcome to this powerful journey of building resilience through the foundation of your self-worth.

Workbook Lesson: Day 15 - Defining Self-Worth

Embracing Your Inherent Value: Defining Self-Worth in God's Truth

Self-worth is not something earned through achievements or the opinions of others, but rather an inherent value given by God. Defining self-worth means recognizing that your value comes from being created in God's image, as stated in *Psalm 139:14, "I praise you because I am fearfully and wonderfully made."* Your worth is not dependent on success, possessions, or external validation. Instead, it stems from the simple truth that you are loved, valued, and chosen by God, regardless of your imperfections or past mistakes. Understanding this allows you to build a foundation of confidence, rooted in the knowledge that your worth is unchanging in God's eyes, which strengthens your ability to face life's challenges with grace and resilience.

As you reflect on your self-worth, take time to identify how external factors may have shaped your self-perception. ***Romans 12:2*** reminds us to ***"not conform to the pattern of this world, but be transformed by the renewing of your mind."*** This scripture invites you to let go of false beliefs that may have diminished your sense of value and to embrace the truth of your worth in Christ. By defining and accepting your self-worth through the lens of God's love, you open yourself to greater self-love, empowerment, and the ability to set healthy boundaries that reflect the respect and dignity God desires for you. This journey is not about perfection but about recognizing that, in God's eyes, you are worthy of love, grace, and acceptance, no matter the circumstances.

Purpose:

The purpose of today's lesson is to help you reflect on and

define what self-worth means to you personally. Understanding your value is the foundation for building resilience, confidence, and lasting change.

Introduction:

Self-worth is the belief that you are inherently valuable, regardless of external factors such as achievements, opinions, or past mistakes. Your worth is not determined by what you do but by who you are. Today's reflection will guide you to explore what self-worth means to you on a personal and spiritual level. By connecting with the truth of your value in God's eyes, you can begin to build a solid foundation that strengthens your resilience.

Reflection Exercise:

1. **Define your self-worth:** Take a few moments to reflect on what self-worth means to you.

   Journal Prompt: Write down how does it influence the way you view yourself and navigate challenges?

_____

_____

_____

2. **Write down your definition:** Define confidence in your own words, considering how it feels and what it looks like in your daily life.

   Journal Prompt: Write down your definition, focusing on the key elements that contribute to your sense of self-assurance and belief in your abilities.

_____

_____

_____

3. Explore Influences on Self-Worth: Reflect on the various influences that have shaped your understanding of self-worth, such as family, friends, societal expectations, or personal experiences.

Journal Prompt: Write about specific influences that have impacted your perception of self-worth. How have these influences affected your self-image, and what steps can you take to align your understanding of self-worth with God's truth rather than external validation?

_____

_____

_____

Reflection Question:

How does recognizing your self-worth contribute to developing a stronger and more resilient mindset?

Journal Prompt: Write about a time when you acknowledged your self-worth and how it positively impacted your mindset during a challenging situation. Reflect on how this understanding of your worth can serve as a foundation for resilience in future challenges.

_____

_____

_____

Day 15 – Conclusion: Embracing Your God-Given Worth

Defining your self-worth in light of God's truth is a transformative step in building a resilient mindset. When you understand that your value is not determined by external achievements or the opinions of others, but by the fact that you are fearfully and wonderfully made (***Psalm 139:14***), you can release the need for constant validation and embrace your inherent worth. This foundation allows you to navigate life's challenges with grace, knowing that your value in God's eyes remains constant, no matter what. As you continue this journey, let ***Romans 12:2*** guide you in renewing your mind, freeing yourself from the false beliefs of the world, and embracing the truth of your worth in Christ. By anchoring your self-worth in God's unchanging love, you empower yourself to set healthy boundaries, love yourself more fully, and face the future with confidence and resilience.

Workbook Lesson: Day 16 - Boundaries for Healthy Self-Worth

Establishing Boundaries to Honor Your God-Given Worth

Boundaries are essential for honoring the self-worth that God has placed within you. ***Proverbs 4:23*** (NIV) reminds us to ***"Above all else, guard your heart, for everything you do flows from it."*** Setting boundaries allows you to guard your emotional, mental, and spiritual well-being, ensuring that your relationships and interactions align with God's purpose for your life. By creating healthy boundaries, you communicate your value as someone created in God's image, deserving of love and respect. Without these boundaries, it becomes easy to compromise your well-being for the sake of pleasing others or avoiding conflict. However, establishing clear guidelines for how you want to be treated strengthens your self-worth and creates a safe space for you to thrive.

Establishing boundaries also allows you to live out the principle of loving others without losing yourself. ***Ephesians 4:15*** (NIV) encourages us ***to "speak the truth in love,"*** which includes expressing our needs and setting limits when necessary. Boundaries are not about distancing yourself from others, but about fostering healthy, God-honoring relationships built on mutual respect. Whether it's learning to say "no" when needed, distancing yourself from toxic behaviors, or simply making time for rest and self-care, boundaries help you walk in the fullness of God's purpose for your life. As you practice setting boundaries, you will grow in confidence, knowing that your self-worth is rooted in God's love and your life is aligned with His will.

Purpose:

Today's lesson focuses on the importance of setting boundaries to maintain and enhance your self-worth. Healthy boundaries are essential for protecting your emotional and mental well-being.

Introduction:

Boundaries are a reflection of how you value yourself and your time. They help you create space to protect your emotional health and prevent others from taking advantage of your kindness or energy. By setting clear boundaries, you are affirming your self-worth and building resilience. Boundaries are not walls but guides that support healthy relationships and self-respect.

Reflection Exercise:

1. **Identify areas where you need stronger boundaries:** Reflect on areas of your life where you feel drained or disrespected.

   Journal Prompt: Write down areas where you need stronger boundaries.

   _____

   _____

   _____

2. **Set clear boundaries:** For each area, create a boundary that protects your well-being. Practice communicating these boundaries with love and confidence.

   Journal Prompt: Write down your creative boundaries that protect you.

   _____

   _____

   _____

Reflection Question:

How do boundaries enhance your sense of self-worth and support emotional resilience?

   Journal Prompt: Write down how setting boundaries has influenced your sense of self-worth and emotional resilience.

   _____

   _____

   _____

Day 16 - Conclusion: Strengthening Your Self-Worth Through Boundaries

Establishing healthy boundaries is an essential step toward protecting and honoring your God-given worth. By setting boundaries, you are guarding your heart, as ***Proverbs 4:23*** (NIV) instructs, allowing you to nurture your emotional, mental, and spiritual well-being. Boundaries are not barriers; rather, they are expressions of self-respect and love that create space for you to thrive and foster meaningful, God-honoring relationships. As you set clear guidelines for how you allow others to treat you, you are affirming the truth that you are fearfully and wonderfully made, deserving of respect and care.

By practicing boundaries in your life, you are living out ***Ephesians 4:15*** (NIV), speaking the truth in love and honoring both yourself and others. Whether it's learning to say "no," protecting your time, or stepping away from toxic influences, boundaries empower you to live confidently in alignment with God's will. As you move forward, remember that your self-worth is not based on others' opinions or external validation, but on the unchanging truth of who you are in Christ. Boundaries will help you maintain this sense of worth and walk in the fullness of God's purpose for your life.

Workbook Lesson: Day 17 - Forgiving Yourself

Embracing Grace: The Power of Self-Forgiveness

Forgiving yourself is a crucial step in the healing process and in building a healthy sense of self-worth. Often, we hold onto guilt, shame, or regret for mistakes we've made, which can weigh us down and prevent us from moving forward. Yet, as we are reminded in *1 John 1:9* (NIV), ***"If we confess our sins, He is faithful and just and will forgive us our sins and purify us from all unrighteousness."*** Just as God forgives us, we must learn to extend that same grace and forgiveness to ourselves. Holding onto past mistakes only hinders our growth, while self-forgiveness frees us to embrace healing, renewal, and a fresh start.

In forgiving yourself, you acknowledge that you are human and, like everyone else, you are not perfect. Mistakes arc a natural part of life and an opportunity for learning and growth. By releasing the guilt and shame associated with past mistakes, you open your heart to healing and allow God's grace to work in your life. This process is not about excusing poor choices or dismissing their impact but about recognizing that you are not defined by your past. By forgiving yourself, you choose to see yourself through God's eyes—worthy of love, healing, and new beginnings.

As you move forward in your journey of self-forgiveness, remember that true forgiveness is an act of self-compassion. It is about letting go of the heavy burden that guilt places on your heart and choosing to walk in the freedom that comes from grace. In *Ephesians 4:32* (NIV), we are encouraged to *"be kind and compassionate to one another, forgiving each other, just as in Christ God forgave you."* This includes being kind and compassionate to yourself. By practicing self-forgiveness, you strengthen your self-worth and build a foundation for lasting resilience, knowing that you are a work in progress, loved, and constantly growing in God's grace.

Purpose:

This lesson helps you explore the healing power of self-forgiveness. By forgiving yourself, you free yourself from the burden of guilt and shame, allowing room for growth and resilience.

Introduction:

Forgiveness is often associated with others, but self-forgiveness is just as important. Holding onto guilt or regret can weaken your sense of self-worth and prevent you from moving forward. Today, you will reflect on the areas where you need to extend forgiveness to yourself. Through self-forgiveness, you release the past and embrace healing, which strengthens your emotional resilience.

Reflection Exercise:

1. Identify areas of self-forgiveness:

Journal Prompt: Write down any situations or past actions where you struggle to forgive yourself.

_____

_____

_____

2. Practice releasing guilt:

Journal Prompt: Write a forgiveness statement for yourself, releasing any negative emotions tied to the past.

_____

_____

_____

Reflection Question:

How does forgiving yourself create space for emotional healing and resilience?

Journal Prompt: Write down in your journal how forgiving yourself create emotional healing.

_____

_____

_____

Day 17 - Conclusion: Releasing Guilt: Walking in Freedom through Self-Forgiveness

As we conclude Day 17 on the importance of self-forgiveness, it becomes clear that letting go of past guilt and shame is an essential step in building self-worth and emotional resilience. Self-forgiveness is not about dismissing your mistakes but acknowledging that you, like everyone else, are human and capable of growth. By embracing God's grace and extending that same grace to yourself, you create space for healing and renewal. In *1 John 1:9*, we are reminded that God is faithful and just to forgive us, and by accepting this forgiveness, you free yourself from the heavy burden of guilt and step into the fresh start that God offers you.

True self-forgiveness strengthens your emotional resilience by allowing you to move forward with compassion, not only for others but also for yourself. As you walk in this freedom, remember *Ephesians 4:32*, which encourages us to be kind and compassionate, even toward ourselves. By releasing the grip of past mistakes, you open the door to greater self-love, growth, and the realization that you are a work in progress, loved and valued by God. This journey of self-forgiveness is not just a path to healing; it's a path to embracing the fullness of life that God desires for you.

Workbook Lesson: Day 18 - Practicing Self-Compassion

Nurturing Yourself with Grace: The Practice of Self-Compassion

Practicing self-compassion means treating yourself with the same kindness and understanding that you would offer to someone you care about. Often, we are much harsher on ourselves than we are on others, holding ourselves to unrealistic standards and criticizing every perceived mistake. Self-compassion invites us to embrace our imperfections, recognizing that we are human and deserving of grace. In *Matthew 22:39* (NIV), Jesus teaches, ***"Love your neighbor as yourself."*** This verse reminds us that self-compassion is not only about how we treat others but also about how we treat ourselves. By offering ourselves kindness and forgiveness, we create space for healing, growth, and inner peace.

When you practice self-compassion, you build a foundation of emotional resilience. Instead of being weighed down by self-criticism or harsh judgments, you begin to approach your challenges with patience and understanding. This shift in perspective helps you see setbacks as opportunities for learning rather than failures. Self-compassion doesn't mean avoiding accountability or ignoring areas for improvement. Instead, it allows you to face life's difficulties with a more balanced mindset, knowing that your worth is not determined by perfection, but by the love and grace that God has for you. Through this practice, you nurture a more positive and supportive relationship with yourself, which strengthens your overall well-being and self-worth.

Purpose:

Today's focus is on developing a daily practice of self-compassion, which is essential for nurturing self-worth and emotional resilience.

Introduction:

Self-compassion involves treating yourself with the same kindness and understanding that you would offer a close friend. It means accepting your imperfections and mistakes without harsh judgment. By practicing self-compassion daily, you strengthen your sense of worth and develop greater emotional resilience. Self-kindness creates a supportive inner environment that allows you to bounce back from challenges with grace.

Reflection Exercise:

1. Practice self-compassion: Each time you notice self-criticism today, pause and reframe your thoughts with kindness.

2. Journal your experience:

   Journal Prompt: Write about how practicing self-compassion today affected your mood and outlook.

_____

_____

_____

Reflection Question:

How does self-compassion impact your emotional resilience and sense of self-worth?

   Journal Prompt: Write in your Journal how self-compassion impact you emotionally.

_____

_____

_____

Day 18 – Conclusion: Embracing Kindness: The Impact of Self-Compassion

As we conclude Day 18 on practicing self-compassion, we recognize the profound impact this practice has on our emotional resilience and self-worth. When we treat ourselves with the same kindness we extend to others, we create space for healing and growth. Self-compassion allows us to embrace our imperfections without harsh judgment, understanding that we are human and deserving of grace. ***In Matthew 22:39*** (NIV), Jesus reminds us to ***"Love your neighbor as yourself,"*** highlighting the importance of offering ourselves the same love and care we give to others. Through self-compassion, we cultivate a balanced perspective on life's challenges, seeing setbacks not as failures but as opportunities to learn and grow in God's grace. By nurturing this compassionate relationship with ourselves, we strengthen our inner peace and build a strong foundation for lasting emotional well-being.

Workbook Lesson: Day 19 - Building Emotional Resilience

Strengthening Through Faith: Cultivating Emotional Resilience

Emotional resilience is the ability to navigate life's challenges, setbacks, and stresses with strength and adaptability. It's not about avoiding difficult emotions or pretending they don't exist; instead, it's about learning how to cope with them in healthy ways. Emotional resilience allows you to face adversity without being overwhelmed by it, bouncing back from hardships with greater wisdom and strength. One key aspect of building emotional resilience is grounding yourself in your faith and trusting that you are never alone, even in the darkest moments. ***Philippians 4:13*** (NIV) reminds us, ***"I can do all this through Him who gives me strength."*** This scripture offers reassurance that through God's strength, we have the power to face any obstacle and grow from it.

To cultivate emotional resilience, it is essential to recognize the role that your self-worth plays in your ability to cope with difficulties. When you understand your value and believe that you are worthy of love and respect, you are better equipped to handle life's ups and downs without being defined by them. Self-worth gives you the confidence to face challenges head-on, knowing that your identity is not shaken by temporary hardships. Resilient people are able to acknowledge their emotions, process them, and still move forward, trusting that growth is possible even in times of struggle. By practicing emotional resilience, you strengthen your ability to navigate change and uncertainty while maintaining a sense of stability and inner peace.

Building emotional resilience also involves embracing the support of others. No one is meant to go through life's challenges alone, and resilience is often fostered through community and relationships. Just as God strengthens us, He also places people in our lives to encourage and uplift us. By relying on the strength of our faith, our inner self-worth, and the support of others, we can develop the emotional resilience necessary to thrive in both good times and bad. Through this resilience, you can face the future with hope and confidence, trusting in God's unfailing love to guide you through every circumstance.

Purpose:

The goal of this lesson is to help you develop emotional strength by connecting your self-worth with resilience.

Introduction:

Emotional resilience allows you to bounce back from difficult experiences without losing your sense of self-worth. It involves maintaining your inner stability and peace even when faced with adversity. Today's reflection focuses on how emotional resilience grows when you are rooted in the belief that your worth does not depend on external circumstances. Building emotional strength helps you remain grounded, no matter what life throws your way.

Reflection Exercise:

1. Reflect on past challenges:

   Journal Prompt: Write about a difficult time in your life where you demonstrated emotional resilience.

   _____

   _____

   _____

2. Identify growth: How did your belief in your own worth help you overcome that challenge?

   Journal Prompt: Write down your belief of your own worth.

   _____

   _____

   _____

Reflection Question:

How does strengthening your emotional resilience help you maintain a sense of self-worth during tough times?

> *Journal Prompt:* Write how does strengthening your emotional resilience help you.

Day 19 – Conclusion: Grounded in Faith: Building Lasting Emotional Resilience

As we conclude Chapter 19 on building emotional resilience, it's important to recognize that resilience is not about avoiding difficulties but about learning how to navigate through them with faith and strength. By grounding yourself in God's promises, such as *Philippians 4:13, "I can do all this through*

Him who gives me strength," you empower yourself to face adversity with confidence and adaptability. Emotional resilience is built on the foundation of understanding your self-worth and trusting that no challenge can define or diminish your value. As you continue to grow in resilience, remember that your worth is not dictated by external circumstances but by the unwavering love of God.

By practicing emotional resilience, you become more capable of bouncing back from life's trials with a sense of stability and inner peace. Leaning on your faith and the support of others, you are able to process emotions in a healthy way and move forward with strength. Embracing the growth that comes from hardship, you cultivate the emotional resilience necessary to thrive, knowing that God's love and purpose are your firm foundation through all of life's ups and downs.

Workbook Lesson: Day 20 - Developing Mental Toughness

Harnessing Strength: Cultivating Mental Toughness

Developing mental toughness is about cultivating the inner strength to persevere through life's challenges, staying focused on your goals even when faced with adversity. It involves pushing through discomfort, fear, and uncertainty with a mindset of growth, recognizing that each obstacle presents an opportunity to build character and resilience. *Philippians 4:13* (NIV) reminds us, *"I can do all this through Him who gives me strength,"* emphasizing that our mental toughness is not about going through life alone but relying on God's strength to guide us through difficulties. By grounding yourself in faith, you can face challenges with the confidence that God's power is at work within you, helping you navigate even the toughest of times.

An important element of mental toughness is maintaining focus and discipline, especially when situations feel overwhelming. This requires setting clear boundaries, practicing self-compassion, and trusting the journey even when progress seems slow. *Hebrews 12:1* (NIV) encourages us to *"run with perseverance the race marked out for us,"* highlighting the importance of staying committed to your purpose, no matter the hurdles you encounter. By cultivating mental toughness, you create a foundation of stability and resilience, allowing you to move forward with clarity and strength, rooted in the assurance that God is with you every step of the way.

Purpose:

Today's lesson focuses on strategies for developing mental toughness, which is essential for a resilient mindset.

Introduction:

Mental toughness is the ability to face challenges with confidence and determination. It involves perseverance, focus, and the belief that you are capable of overcoming obstacles. Mental toughness is built over time and is closely linked to your sense of self-worth. When you believe in your value, you are more likely to face difficulties with confidence and resilience.

Reflection Exercise:

1. Identify mental blocks:

    Journal Prompt: Write down any current mental blocks
    or fears that are holding you back

    _____

    _____

    _____

2. Create an action plan:

    Journal Prompt: Develop a plan to overcome these
    blocks by using mental strategies such as positive self-
    talk, visualization, and goal setting.

    _____

    _____

    _____

Reflection Question:

How does mental toughness help you stay resilient in the face of adversity?

> *Journal Prompt:* Reflect on a time when you faced a difficult situation and drew upon your mental toughness to navigate it. How did your resilience shape the way you responded, and what lessons did you learn about your own strength in the process?

_____

_____

_____

Day 20 – Conclusion: Harnessing Strength Through Faith: Building Mental Toughness

As we conclude Chapter 20 on developing mental toughness, it's clear that cultivating inner strength is essential for overcoming life's challenges with resilience and determination.

Mental toughness involves staying focused on your goals, pushing through discomfort, and trusting that God's strength will guide you through adversity. As ***Philippians 4:13*** (NIV) reminds us, ***"I can do all this through Him who gives me strength,"*** mental toughness is not just about personal willpower but about relying on God's power to carry you forward. By grounding your perseverance in faith, you develop the clarity and confidence needed to navigate even the toughest obstacles with grace.

Maintaining mental toughness also requires focus and discipline, staying committed to your purpose despite the distractions and difficulties life may present. ***Hebrews 12:1*** (NIV) encourages us to "run with perseverance the race marked out for us," underscoring the importance of persistence and determination. Through this chapter, you've learned that mental toughness is not about perfection but about embracing the process of growth, knowing that every challenge is an opportunity to build character and resilience. With God by your side, you can confidently face any adversity, knowing that His strength will sustain you.

Workbook Lesson: Day 21 - Anchoring in Self-Worth

Rooted in God's Love: Anchoring in True Self-Worth

Anchoring in self-worth means deeply rooting yourself in the truth of your intrinsic value, recognizing that your worth is not contingent on external achievements, opinions, or circumstances. True self-worth arises from understanding your unique qualities and the purpose for which you were created. Anchoring in this awareness allows you to withstand challenges with greater resilience because your foundation is solid. As *Isaiah 43:4* (NIV) reminds us, ***"Since you are precious and honored in my sight, and because I love you."*** Knowing that you are precious in God's eyes gives you the strength to stand firm in your worth, regardless of what life throws your way.

Rejecting the false identities and labels others have placed on you is key to anchoring in your self-worth. Whether these labels come from past experiences, relationships, or your own negative self-talk, they often undermine your confidence and distort your perception of your value. Instead, focus on what is true—God's love for you, your unique strengths, and your capacity for growth and transformation. Anchoring yourself in these truths provides the inner strength needed to face setbacks with grace, knowing that no failure or challenge can diminish your worth. This mindset allows you to embrace life's difficulties as opportunities for growth, secure in the knowledge that you are worthy and capable.

As you reflect on how your understanding of self-worth has evolved throughout this chapter, consider how this foundation continues to support your emotional and mental resilience. When your self-worth is deeply anchored, you are empowered to set healthy boundaries, practice self-compassion, and face life's challenges with renewed confidence. This unwavering sense of worth equips you to approach your journey with clarity and purpose, knowing that every step forward is grounded in your true value. By continuing to nurture and strengthen your self-worth, you ensure that your growth is sustainable and that the changes you seek will have lasting impact.

Purpose:

Today's lesson is about reflecting on how your understanding of self-worth has evolved and how it supports your resilience.

Introduction:

As you complete this week's reflections, take time to anchor yourself in the truth of your worth. Your self-worth is not only the foundation of your resilience but also the key to lasting change. Today, you will reflect on how your journey of building resilience has transformed the way you see yourself. By anchoring in self-worth, you create a stable foundation that supports your continued growth.

Reflection Exercise:

1. Reflect on your journey:

Journal Prompt: Write about how your understanding of self-worth has evolved over the past week.

_____

_____

_____

2. Set intentions:

   Journal Prompt: Write down two ways you will continue to strengthen your self-worth and resilience moving forward.

_____

_____

_____

Reflection Question:

How does anchoring in your self-worth support your long-term resilience and growth?

Journal Prompt: Write about how anchoring in this truth of your worth can continue to shape your future, guiding you to face adversity with confidence and embrace new opportunities for growth.

_____

_____

_____

Day 21 – Conclusion: Grounded in God's Truth: The Power of Anchoring in Self-Worth

As you conclude Day 21, anchoring in your self-worth means deeply recognizing that your value is rooted in God's love, not in external achievements or the opinions of others. *Isaiah 43:4* reminds us that you are *"precious and honored"* in God's sight, which provides a firm foundation for building lasting resilience. By rejecting false labels and embracing your true identity in Christ, you equip yourself to face life's challenges with grace and confidence. Anchoring self-worth empowers you to set healthy boundaries, practice self-compassion, and see setbacks as opportunities for growth. Moving forward, continue to nurture this strong foundation, knowing that your worth is unshakable and grounded in God's unchanging love.

Activity:

Resilience Rooted in Self-Worth

Objective:

This activity is designed to help you solidify your understanding of self-worth and develop a practical strategy for building emotional and mental resilience. By connecting your self-worth to the resilience, you need to navigate life's challenges, this activity will encourage you to reflect, set boundaries, and create affirmations that support your journey toward lasting change.

Step 1: Personal Reflection on Self-Worth (10 minutes)

- Take 10 minutes to sit quietly and reflect on how you currently view your self-worth. What beliefs have shaped your sense of worth up to this point? Have external factors such as achievements, opinions, or past mistakes influenced your self-worth in positive or negative ways?

- Write down a list of qualities that you believe define your true worth. Include qualities like kindness, resilience, creativity, or compassion—qualities that remain consistent, regardless of external factors.

Journal Prompt:

_____

_____

_____

Step 2: Boundaries to Protect Your Self-Worth (15 minutes)

- Boundaries are essential for maintaining and strengthening self-worth. Take a few moments to identify areas of your life where you've struggled to set clear boundaries, whether it's with work, relationships, or self-care.

Exercise:

- Write down 2-3 boundaries that you need to set in these areas to protect your emotional and mental well-being. For example, one boundary might be "I will not overextend myself at work beyond my capacity" or "I will say no to commitments that drain my energy."

  Journal Prompt:

  _____

  _____

  _____

- How will setting these boundaries help reinforce your sense of worth and protect your resilience in the face of challenges?

Journal Prompt:

_____

_____

_____

Step 3: Create Affirmations for Resilience (10 minutes)

- Using the self-worth qualities, you wrote earlier, create 3-5 personal affirmations that reflect your inner strength and resilience. For example, "I am worthy of love and respect," or "I have the strength to face any challenge with grace."

Exercise:

- Write these affirmations on a note card or in your journal. Place them somewhere visible so you can read and repeat them daily, reminding yourself of your inherent worth and the resilience you possess.

Journal Prompt:

_____

_____

_____

Step 4: Visualization Exercise (5 minutes)

- Close your eyes and visualize yourself in a challenging situation. See yourself responding with calm, resilience, and confidence, anchored in the truth of your self-worth. Imagine that every setback is an opportunity for growth and every obstacle strengthens your resolve.

Reflection:

- Write down how did this visualization help you see yourself as resilient, capable, and worthy, regardless of external circumstances?

Journal Prompt:

_____

_____

_____

Step 5: Reflection and Intention Setting (5 minutes)

- Now that you've reflected on your self-worth, set boundaries, and created affirmations, take a moment to write down one specific area in your life where you want to apply these principles. How will your new understanding of self-worth and resilience help you in this area?

- In what ways do you anticipate that building resilience through self-worth will positively impact your future challenges? Write down how you continue to reinforce your self-worth daily?

Journal Prompt:

_____

_____

Bonus Step: Create a Resilience Map

- On a piece of paper or digitally, create a "Resilience Map." Draw connections between your self-worth qualities, affirmations, and boundaries. Visually map out how these elements support each other to create a strong, resilient mindset. This map serves as a reminder of how deeply your self-worth is tied to your ability to navigate life's challenges.

Reflection Question:

- How does anchoring in your self-worth strengthen your resilience and empower you to face challenges with confidence and peace?

Journal Prompt:

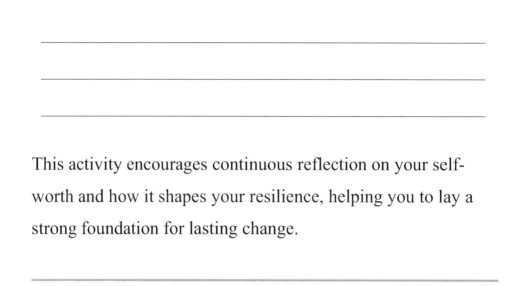

This activity encourages continuous reflection on your self-worth and how it shapes your resilience, helping you to lay a strong foundation for lasting change.

Conclusion for Chapter 3: Building Resilience Through Self-Worth

As you reach the conclusion of Chapter 3, "Building Resilience Through Self-Worth," you've gained a deeper understanding of how your self-worth is foundational in creating lasting resilience. Throughout Days 15-21, you have explored defining your self-worth, establishing boundaries, practicing self-compassion, and developing both emotional resilience and mental toughness. Each of these elements has served to strengthen your ability to face challenges with grace, confidence, and determination. By anchoring yourself in your inherent value, you have laid the groundwork for enduring resilience, which empowers you to navigate life's trials with steady faith and perseverance.

Building resilience through self-worth isn't just about recognizing your value—it's about understanding that your worth comes from God. In *Isaiah 43:4*, God tells us, *"Since you are precious and honored in my sight, and because I love you."* This truth anchors us during difficult times, reminding us that no matter what happens, our worth is secure in His love. Whether it's learning to set boundaries that protect your well-being or forgiving yourself for past mistakes, each step has brought you closer to becoming the resilient person God has called you to be.

Moving forward, continue to build on the practices you've developed in this chapter. Remember, resilience is a journey that requires consistent nurturing of your self-worth and faith in God's plan. *Philippians 4:13* reminds us, *"I can do all this through Him who gives me strength. "* Let this scripture continue to guide you as you face future challenges, knowing that your strength and resilience are rooted in God's love and your unshakable sense of self-worth.

Reflection Question: How has strengthening your self-worth through resilience helped you to see challenges as opportunities for growth rather than setbacks?

Journal Prompt:

_____

_____

_____

Weekly Prayer for the end of Chapter 3: Building Resilience Through Self-Worth

Heavenly Father,

I come before You today, grateful for the strength and resilience You have placed within me. Help me to see myself through Your eyes, knowing that my worth is not determined by circumstances or the opinions of others, but by Your unfailing love. Grant me the grace to forgive myself, set healthy boundaries, and walk confidently in the truth of who I am in You. Lord, I trust in Your strength to guide me through every challenge I face, knowing that I can do all things through You who give me strength.

In Jesus' name, I pray Amen.

Chapter 4

New Steps: What Is Yours?

Charting Your Path Forward

Days 22-30: Creating New Foundations

Chapter 3, *Building Resilience Through Self-Worth: Strengthening Your Foundation for Lasting Change,* focused on the crucial connection between self-worth and resilience. Throughout Days 15-21, we explored how understanding and embracing your inherent value plays a pivotal role in overcoming challenges and maintaining emotional strength. The lessons covered topics like defining self-worth, setting healthy boundaries, practicing self-compassion, and forgiving yourself. Each concept helped you recognize that your worth is not tied to external circumstances, but rather to your intrinsic value as a person created and loved by God. By anchoring yourself in this truth, you began to develop a resilient mindset that empowers you to face adversity with confidence and grace.

In this chapter, you also learned how to cultivate mental and emotional toughness by reframing challenges as opportunities for growth, trusting in God's strength, and leaning on His promises. *Philippians 4:13* reminds us, *"I can do all things through Him who gives me strength."* This scripture served as a powerful foundation for building resilience, helping you realize that true strength and self-worth come from your relationship with God. As you reflect on this chapter, you can now move forward with greater confidence, knowing that your self-worth provides the foundation for lasting change and the resilience needed to navigate life's ups and downs.

As you enter the final chapter of your journey, you are now prepared to embrace the future with a renewed sense of self-worth and resilience. The path ahead may still hold challenges, but you have been equipped with the tools to navigate them confidently. In this chapter, you will focus on the powerful concept of creating new foundations—building a life that is grounded in the truths you've discovered about yourself. It's a time for reflection and action, where you intentionally step forward and claim the life that is uniquely yours. *Isaiah 43:18-19* reminds us, *"Forget the former things; do not dwell on the past. See, I am doing a new thing! Now it springs up; do you not perceive it?* I am making a way in the wilderness and streams in the wasteland."* This scripture speaks to the importance of moving beyond the past and embracing the new beginnings God is creating in your life.

Creating new foundations is about acknowledging the growth you've experienced while also committing to a future filled with purpose and intention. The journey you've taken through previous chapters—rewriting your inner dialogue, building resilience through self-worth, and setting healthy boundaries—has prepared you for this pivotal moment. As you chart your path forward, you are not just moving away from the past, but actively shaping a future that aligns with your values, dreams, and God's plan for you. This is the time to reflect on what steps you will take to continue building on the foundations of resilience, faith, and self-worth. It's a time for boldness, guided by the understanding that God is making a new way for you.

Isaiah 43:18-19 invites you to perceive the *"new thing"* that God is doing in your life. Just as God promises to make streams in the wasteland, He is creating pathways for you to thrive in areas where you once felt lost or broken. As you continue to take new steps, bc cncouraged that God is walking with you, guiding each decision and leading you toward His perfect plan. The act of creating new foundations isn't about perfection—it's about remaining open to transformation, allowing God's grace to work through every aspect of your life. Your worth and resilience are deeply rooted in Him, and as you embrace this truth, you are empowered to build a life that reflects His love, strength, and purpose.

In these final days, consider how you will continue to cultivate your new mindset and strengthen the foundations you've laid. What specific steps will you take to ensure that your progress is sustained? How will you continue to anchor yourself in God's promises and His vision for your life? Reflect on the lessons you've learned throughout this journey and trust that the new foundations you're creating will support the life of growth, healing, and purpose that God has for you. Embrace this chapter as an opportunity to move forward with confidence, knowing that every step you take is part of the greater journey that God has planned for you.

Weekly Prayer for Chapter 4: Embracing New Foundations and Reflecting on Growth

Heavenly Father,

I come before You with gratitude for the lessons and growth that have shaped my hearts and mind throughout this journey. As I reflect on Chapters 1, 2, and 3, I thank You for guiding me through the process of self-discovery, healing, and transformation. In Chapter 1, I learned the power of acknowledging my emotions and recognizing where I stand. In Chapter 2, I embraced the courage to rewrite my inner dialogue, replacing negative self-talk with affirmations grounded in Your truth. And in Chapter 3, I discovered the deep connection between self-worth and resilience, building a foundation that allows me to face challenges with grace and confidence. Thank You for walking with me every step of the way, filling me with strength, love, and self-compassion as I grow.

As I enter Chapter 4 and begin creating new foundations, I ask for Your continued guidance and wisdom. Help me to step boldly into the future, trusting that You are doing a new thing in my life, just as *Isaiah 43:18-19* promises. Let my heart be open to transformation, allowing Your grace to shape my path forward. May I build my life on the truths I have discovered about myself and remain anchored in the self-worth and resilience that come from knowing I am precious in Your sight. Father, I commit this new chapter to You, confident that You will lead me toward healing, growth, and purpose.

In Jesus' name, we pray, Amen

Workbook Lesson Week 4

New Steps: What Is Yours?

Creating New Foundations: Reflecting on Your Growth

As you enter Week 4, you are stepping into a powerful stage of your journey—creating new foundations for your life rooted in the growth, resilience, and self-worth you have developed over the past few weeks. This week is about solidifying the progress you've made by letting go of old patterns and embracing the opportunities that lie ahead. Building new foundations involves reflecting on your journey, identifying the steps you need to take, and setting long-term goals that align with the person you are becoming. With each new foundation, you strengthen your ability to move forward with confidence, resilience, and clarity.

In this final stretch, you will explore key concepts such as embracing new opportunities, setting healthy boundaries, and creating a support network that will help you sustain your progress. By anchoring yourself in these new foundations, you'll be prepared to face future challenges with a renewed sense of purpose and strength. This week marks a significant moment in your healing journey as you begin to walk forward with intention, courage, and trust in the path you are creating. Welcome to the journey of building a future that reflects your true self and the growth you have achieved.

Workbook Lesson: Day 22 - Reflecting on Your Growth

Embracing Your Transformation: Reflecting on the Journey of Growth

As you pause to reflect on your journey, it's important to acknowledge the growth you've experienced, both internally and externally. Growth doesn't happen overnight, and the changes within you are often subtle, taking root slowly over time. Reflecting on your progress allows you to see the beauty in the struggle, the wisdom gained through challenges, and the strength developed in overcoming adversity. Each step you've taken, no matter how small, has led you closer to a more empowered and resilient version of yourself.

As you continue this reflection, recognize how God's grace has been present in every moment. His guidance, love, and support have been the foundation of your growth. Through prayer and faith, you have become stronger, more compassionate, and more aligned with His purpose for your life. This time of reflection is a reminder to celebrate how far you've come and to keep your eyes fixed on the path ahead, trusting that God's hand will continue to lead you toward even greater transformation.

"But grow in the grace and knowledge of our Lord and Savior Jesus Christ. To him be glory both now and forever! Amen."
— 2 Peter 3:18

Purpose:

Today's lesson focuses on taking stock of the progress you've made so far in your healing journey. Reflecting on your growth allows you to acknowledge how far you've come and prepares you for the next steps in your journey.

Introduction:

Growth doesn't happen overnight, but through consistent effort and dedication. It's essential to pause and reflect on the positive changes in your mindset, habits, and emotional resilience. This reflection helps reinforce your progress and gives you the clarity to continue moving forward.

Reflection Exercise:

1. Take a few moments to reflect on specific areas where you've noticed personal growth. Consider how your mindset, resilience, or self-worth has transformed since the beginning of this journey.

Journal Prompt: What positive changes have you experienced, and how have they impacted your daily life?

_____

_____

_____

2. Think about how your faith has grown during this journey. Reflect on any moments where you felt God's presence, guidance, or strength, helping you navigate through challenges.

Journal Prompt: In what ways has your faith strengthened, and how has it influenced your approach to overcoming adversity?

_____

_____

_____

Reflection Question:

How does recognizing your growth inspire you to continue moving forward with faith and confidence?

Journal prompt: Reflect and write down how your progress encourages you to embrace future challenges. What areas do you feel most motivated to continue growing in, and how will you rely on God's strength as you move forward?

Day 22 - Conclusion: Celebrating Your Journey of Growth

As you complete this lesson, take a moment to celebrate the progress you've made. Reflecting on your growth allows you to see the strength and resilience that have carried you through. Each challenge, each victory, and even the smallest breakthrough has played a part in shaping the person you are today. Your healing journey is ongoing but recognizing the steps you've taken so far serves as a powerful reminder of God's grace and your own determination. As you continue forward, carry with you the knowledge that the growth you've embraced will continue to lead you toward even greater transformation. Keep trusting the process and have faith in the amazing journey still unfolding.

Workbook Lesson: Day 23 - Identifying Next Steps

Stepping Forward with Purpose: Identifying the Path Ahead

As you move forward in your healing journey, identifying the next steps is crucial to maintaining your growth and building upon the progress you've already made. This process involves taking a thoughtful look at where you are now, recognizing the areas in which you've grown and pinpointing where you want to go next. Your next steps should be aligned with your values, personal goals, and the new understanding of your self-worth. By focusing on intentional actions, you create a clear path forward that supports your continued development and emotional well-being. *"The steps of a good man are ordered by the Lord, and He delights in his way." — Psalm 37:23.* This verse reminds us that each step you take is guided by

God's hand, ensuring that your path is aligned with His purpose for your life.

Defining your next steps doesn't mean overwhelming yourself with drastic changes all at once. Instead, think of these steps as small, manageable actions that lead to significant transformation over time. Perhaps it involves setting healthy boundaries in relationships, committing to a daily self-care routine, or seeking new opportunities that reflect your newfound confidence. Whatever your next steps may be, they should reflect your desire to continue growing, healing, and nurturing your self-worth. With God directing your steps, you can trust that He is shaping your journey toward a life that reflects the strength, resilience, and value you are discovering within yourself.

Purpose:

Today's focus is on defining the new steps that will continue your growth. By identifying clear next steps, you will have a roadmap to guide you as you build new foundations for your life.

Introduction:

Growth is an ongoing process. Now that you've reflected on how far you've come, it's time to plan for your future. Think about the areas where you want to continue growing and healing.

Reflection Exercise:

1. Reflect on the areas of your life where you feel the most growth and alignment with your values. Think about how these areas can be nurtured as you move forward and what next steps will help reinforce this progress.

   Journal Prompt: Which areas of growth do you feel most proud of, and how can you continue to build on these strengths in the next phase of your journey?

   How will these steps contribute to your continued healing and development?

_____

_____

_____

Journal *Prompt:* What are your new steps, and how will they build upon the progress you've made?

_____

_____

_____

Reflection Question:

How does aligning your next steps with your values and faith reinforce your commitment to growth and healing?

Journal Prompt: Reflect on how grounding your future steps in both personal values and faith can deepen your sense of purpose and resilience. What steps will you take to ensure that your actions align with these principles?

_____

_____

_____

Day 23 – Conclusion: Embracing the Journey of Continuous Growth

As you conclude this lesson, take heart in knowing that each step you identify is a powerful commitment to your continued healing and development. The process of identifying next steps is not only about looking forward but also about recognizing that God is guiding you toward His perfect plan for your life. By aligning your next steps with your values and goals, you are actively creating a roadmap that honors your growth and self-worth. These steps may be small, but they hold the potential for significant transformation over time. Trust that with each new step, you are moving closer to the person you are becoming—a person of strength, resilience, and purpose.

As you embark on this next phase of your journey, remember to approach it with patience and grace. Growth is an ongoing process, and each new action you take is a testament to your commitment to healing and building a life rooted in confidence and faith. Let this be a reminder that God is walking with you, guiding every step, as you continue to evolve and embrace the fullness of who He has called you to be.

Workbook Lesson: Day 24 - Letting Go of the Past

Releasing the Past: Embracing Freedom and New Beginnings

Letting go of the past is a powerful step in breaking free from the patterns of hurt that keep us bound to old wounds. It doesn't mean forgetting or dismissing what has happened but choosing to release the emotional grip the past holds over your present and future. This process invites you to release resentment, anger, or pain tied to specific experiences, recognizing that these no longer define who you are. Letting go is an act of liberation, allowing you to move beyond the emotional weight that prevents you from fully stepping into the person you are becoming. As Jesus said, *"Come to me, all who labor and are heavy laden, and I will give you rest."* (*Matthew 11:28*). His promise reminds us that we can surrender our burdens to Him and find peace in the process of release.

As you let go, you create space for healing and new possibilities to unfold. This act of release opens the door to healthier relationships, greater self-worth, and a future aligned with your true values and desires. It allows you to view your past not as a chain holding you back but as a part of your story that has shaped you, even as you choose to move forward. While the journey of letting go may come with challenges, it is essential in cultivating a life rooted in clarity, peace, and growth.

By choosing to release the past, you reclaim your power and step into a future filled with hope and renewal. It is in this act of letting go that you embrace the freedom to rewrite your narrative, no longer defined by old fears or painful memories. Trust that as you walk this path, God is guiding you toward new beginnings, stronger foundations, and a life filled with compassion, purpose, and grace.

Purpose:

This lesson helps you explore strategies to release old habits, thoughts, or people that no longer serve your healing journey. Letting go is essential to create space for growth and new beginnings.

Introduction:

Sometimes, holding onto the past can weigh you down and hinder your progress. Letting go is not about forgetting, but about freeing yourself from what no longer serves your growth.

Reflection Exercise:

1. Take a moment to think of an experience from your past that still lingers in your heart. Consider how holding onto this hurt impacts your present well-being and what it would feel like to release it.

   Journal Prompt: What emotions come up when you think about letting go of this past hurt, and how do you imagine freedom from it would change your daily life?

   _____

   _____

   _____

2. Close your eyes and imagine a future where you have fully let go of any lingering pain or regret. Visualize yourself living without the weight of past burdens and focus on the joy and peace this brings.

Journal Prompt: What would your life look like if you no longer carried the weight of your past, and what positive changes do you think would unfold?

_____

_____

_____

Reflection Question

How does letting go of the past open the door to a future filled with new opportunities and growth?

Journal Prompt: Reflect and write down how releasing past struggles can help you embrace new possibilities and create a life that reflects your true values. What steps will you take to ensure your future is guided by peace and purpose?

_____

_____

_____

Day 24 – Conclusion: Stepping Into a Future of Healing and Growth

As you complete this lesson on letting go of the past, recognize the power that comes with release. By loosening the emotional grip of old wounds, you are making space for new—new opportunities, healthier relationships, and a future rooted in healing. Letting go allows you to reclaim your power and embrace the freedom to move forward with clarity and purpose. Though this process may be challenging, each step you take toward release is a step toward a life filled with hope, renewal, and growth. Trust that God is walking beside you, guiding you into a future that reflects His grace and love.

Workbook Lesson: Day 25 - Embracing New Opportunities

Stepping Boldly Into New Possibilities

Embracing new opportunities is a crucial step in your journey toward healing and growth. After letting go of the past and shedding the limiting beliefs or relationships that once held you back, you open yourself to new possibilities that align with your true self. These opportunities can come in many forms— whether they involve pursuing personal goals, stepping into healthier relationships, or exploring areas of life you've previously avoided due to fear or self-doubt. By embracing what's ahead, you create room for personal growth, fulfillment, and a renewed sense of purpose. It's an empowering process that requires courage, faith, and a willingness to explore the unknown.

The key to embracing new opportunities is to approach them with an open heart and mind. This often means being willing to take risks, challenge your comfort zone, and trusting that you are capable of handling what comes your way. The growth you've experienced thus far has equipped you to face these new possibilities with confidence, and each opportunity you embrace allows you to expand your understanding of yourself and the world around you. It is through seizing these moments that you can fully step into the life you desire—one that reflects your worth, values, and aspirations.

While embracing new opportunities can feel intimidating, it's important to remember that these moments are part of your ongoing journey of transformation. Each new step is a chance to build upon the foundations you've already established, helping you move further away from past limitations and closer to a future of abundance and self-empowerment. Embrace these opportunities as invitations to grow, knowing that with every step forward, you are creating a life that aligns with your truest self and aspirations.

Purpose:

Today's lesson focuses on opening yourself up to new opportunities that align with your self-worth. Embracing new possibilities can enhance your growth and bring positive change into your life.

Introduction:

Growth often requires stepping outside of your comfort zone and embracing new opportunities. These opportunities can help you align with your true self and continue to build your confidence.

Reflection Exercise:

1. Reflect on an opportunity that recently presented itself and think about what fears or hesitations may have initially held you back from embracing it. Consider what you learned from that experience.

    Journal Prompt: What feelings or thoughts arise when you think about seizing new opportunities, and how can you reframe these to support your growth?

    _____

    _____

2. Identify an area of your life where you feel ready to embrace change or try something new. Reflect on how

embracing this new opportunity aligns with your values and goals.

Journal Prompt: What steps can you take today to welcome new possibilities into your life, and how do they reflect the person you're becoming?

_____

_____

_____

Reflection Question:

How can embracing new opportunities help you continue your journey of self-discovery and personal growth?

Journal Prompt: Reflect on how welcoming new experiences can contribute to a life aligned with your purpose. What kind of opportunities would you like to attract, and how do they reflect your true values?

_____

_____

_____

Day 25 – Conclusion: Embracing Growth Through New Opportunities

As you conclude this lesson, remember that embracing new opportunities is an essential part of your healing journey. Each opportunity you step into allows you to build upon the progress you've already made, pushing past old limitations and stepping into a life filled with possibility. These new experiences, whether personal or relational, are invitations to continue growing, expanding, and aligning more deeply with your true self. Trust that the growth you've achieved so far has equipped you to handle the challenges ahead with confidence, courage, and grace.

While the unknown can feel intimidating, see it as a chance to explore new dimensions of your potential. By approaching each new opportunity with faith and an open heart, you are actively creating a future that reflects your self-worth and aspirations. Let these opportunities serve as steppingstones toward a more empowered and fulfilling life, knowing that you are supported by the foundation you've built and the growth you continue to embrace. Each step forward is an act of self-love, guiding you closer to a life of abundance and purpose.

Workbook Lesson: Day 26 - Setting Long-Term Goals

Charting Your Path: Setting Goals for a Fulfilling Future

Setting long-term goals is an essential part of building a meaningful and fulfilling life, especially as you move forward in your journey of healing and personal growth. Long-term goals provide direction, helping you visualize where you want to be in the future while giving you a sense of purpose and motivation. These goals are not just about achievements but about aligning your actions with your deeper values and aspirations. Whether they pertain to your personal life, relationships, career, or emotional well-being, long-term goals act as guiding principles that keep you focused on what truly matters to you.

As you set these goals, it's important to approach them with a balance of ambition and realism. Start by reflecting on your values, the lessons you've learned in your healing journey, and the areas of your life where you'd like to see continued growth. Then, break down your larger objectives into smaller, actionable steps that are attainable and measurable. This ensures that your long-term goals remain motivating rather than overwhelming. Remember, these goals are flexible and can evolve as you grow—what matters most is that they reflect your evolving sense of self-worth and the future you want to create.

Lastly, setting long-term goals also involves building resilience and commitment. There will inevitably be challenges and setbacks along the way, but having clear goals helps you maintain focus and perseverance. Revisit your goals regularly, celebrating small victories and adjusting your plans as needed. The process of working toward these goals will not only bring you closer to the life you envision but also deepen your sense of purpose and self-confidence. Long-term goals give you a roadmap for growth, helping you stay grounded in your vision for a brighter, more fulfilled future.

Purpose:

This lesson focuses on creating achievable, long-term goals for your personal and emotional development. Setting goals helps provide direction and purpose for your journey forward.

Introduction:

Long-term goals are essential for maintaining momentum in your growth journey. They help you stay focused on what you want to achieve and give you something to work toward.

Reflection Exercise:

1. Write down 2-3 long-term goals for your personal or emotional development.

   Journal Prompt: What specific personal growth goals resonate most with you, and why are they important for your future?

_____

_____

_____

2. Break these goals into smaller, actionable steps you can take in the coming weeks or months.

Journal Prompt: How can breaking down your long-term goals into smaller steps help you maintain focus and celebrate progress along the way?

_____

_____

_____

Reflection Question

How does setting long-term goals create a roadmap for your future growth and fulfillment?

Journal Prompt: Reflect and write down how having clear, long-term goals aligns with your values and inspires you to stay committed to your vision. What strategies will you use to stay focused and adaptable as you work toward these goals?

_____

Day 26 – Conclusion: Staying Committed to Your Vision

As you conclude this lesson on setting long-term goals, remember that these goals are not only about achieving milestones but about creating a meaningful path that aligns with your true self. Long-term goals act as your compass, guiding you toward a future filled with purpose, fulfillment, and continued personal growth. By breaking them into smaller, actionable steps, you make your journey more manageable and less overwhelming. As you pursue these goals, be patient with yourself, knowing that setbacks are part of the process, but each step brings you closer to the life you envision.

Stay committed to revisiting and refining your goals as you grow and evolve. Celebrate your progress along the way and trust that these goals will help you stay focused on what truly matters. With each small victory, you build resilience and confidence, laying the groundwork for a brighter, more empowered future. Let your long-term goals serve as a roadmap, helping you navigate challenges and embrace opportunities with clarity and purpose.

Workbook Lesson: Day 27 - Building a Support Network

Strengthening Your Journey: Building a Supportive Circle

Building a support network is an essential part of sustaining your growth and healing. A strong support system provides encouragement, accountability, and a sense of connection, all of which are crucial as you continue navigating life's challenges. This network can consist of family, friends, mentors, or even professional resources such as therapists or support groups. The people in your network should be individuals who genuinely care about your well-being, uplift you, and offer guidance when needed. Surrounding yourself with positive influences helps you stay focused on your personal goals and ensures that you don't have to face difficult moments alone.

As you build your support network, it's important to seek out people who respect your boundaries, understand your values, and are committed to your journey of healing. This might mean reevaluating certain relationships or distancing yourself from individuals who are unsupportive or draining. Be intentional about fostering connections with those who inspire growth and provide constructive feedback. A healthy support network is a source of strength and stability, empowering you to continue on your path with confidence and resilience, knowing you have people to lean on when needed.

Purpose:

This lesson is about identifying the people who will support you in your continued journey. Having a strong support system is essential for staying resilient and motivated.

Introduction:

No one is meant to journey through healing alone. A support network can offer encouragement, accountability, and understanding as you continue to grow and heal.

Reflection Exercise:

1. Make a list of people in your life who you trust and feel supported by. Reflect on the qualities they bring to your life and how they contribute to your journey of healing. *Journal Prompt:* Who are the people that encourage and support your growth, and what specific qualities do you appreciate most about them?

_____

_____

_____

2. Consider whether there are relationships in your life that may not align with your goals for healing and growth. Reflect on any boundaries you need to set to ensure your support network remains a positive influence.

Journal Prompt: What boundaries might you need to establish to protect your well-being within your support network?

_____

_____

_____

Reflection Question: How does surrounding yourself with a supportive network empower you to stay resilient on your healing journey?

Journal Prompt: Reflect on how your support network influences your resilience. What are some ways they help you stay focused on your personal goals, and how do you plan to nurture these connections moving forward?

_____

_____

_____

Day 27 – Conclusion: Nurturing the Power of Connection

As you conclude this lesson on building a support network, remember that no one heals in isolation. Surrounding yourself with a network of individuals who genuinely care about your well-being is a vital part of your continued growth. These connections provide the strength, encouragement, and accountability you need to stay focused on your goals, while also offering a safe space to lean on during difficult times. By intentionally fostering relationships with those who uplift and inspire you, you're creating a foundation of support that will empower you to navigate life's challenges with resilience and confidence.

As you move forward, recognize that your support network is an evolving part of your healing journey. It's essential to nurture these relationships and ensure they reflect the positive energy and understanding you need. By surrounding yourself with people who respect your boundaries, offer guidance, and share your commitment to growth, you are not only building a circle of support but also reinforcing your own strength. Trust that with this network in place, you are never alone on your path to healing, and that together, you will continue to move toward a life of purpose and fulfillment.

Workbook Lesson: Day 28 - Walking in Your New Confidence

Embracing Strength and Resilience in Every Step

Walking in your new confidence is about embracing the growth, healing, and strength you've cultivated on this journey. Confidence isn't just about outward appearances; it's rooted in your inner belief in your worth, abilities, and potential. You've faced your fears, overcome challenges, and now you stand with a stronger sense of self. This confidence is not fragile but is built on the foundation of your resilience, self-worth, and the lessons you've learned along the way. Walking in your new confidence means stepping into each day with assurance, knowing that you are capable and deserving of the good things that come your way.

As you continue to walk in this confidence, it's important to remember that it doesn't mean you won't face obstacles or moments of doubt. Confidence is not about never feeling unsure; it's about how you respond to those moments with grace and perseverance. When challenges arise, you can trust that you now have the tools to navigate them without losing your sense of self-worth. This confidence is also about standing firm in your boundaries, speaking your truth, and making decisions that align with your values and goals. Each step forward reinforces your belief in yourself and the progress you've made.

Walking in your new confidence also impacts how you engage with the world around you. It influences your relationships, work, and personal pursuits. When you carry yourself with confidence, others notice your sense of purpose and are drawn to your positivity and strength. You become an example of what it looks like to overcome adversity and build a life that reflects your true worth. As you continue this journey, allow your confidence to guide you, opening up new opportunities and empowering you to keep moving forward with courage and conviction.

Purpose:

Today's lesson focuses on reflecting on how your confidence has grown throughout your healing journey and how it will continue to guide you.

Introduction:

Your confidence has evolved as you've learned to embrace your self-worth and release old patterns. Now is the time to reflect on how this confidence will continue to shape your life moving forward.

Reflection Exercise:

1. Reflect on the Impact of Confidence.

   Journal Prompt: How has embracing your confidence changed the way you approach challenges or interact with others?

_____

_____

_____

2. Identify Actions Aligned with Confidence

Journal Prompt: What steps can you take each day to reinforce your confidence and stay true to your self-worth?

_____

_____

_____

Reflection Question

How can walking in your new confidence shape the opportunities you pursue and the relationships you build moving forward?

Journal Prompt: Write down ways that carrying yourself with confidence can impact the choices you make and the way you engage with the world. What goals feel within reach now that you've embraced your inner strength?

_____

_____

_____

Day 28 – Conclusion: Standing Firm in Your Confidence

As you complete this lesson on walking in your new confidence, take a moment to celebrate how far you've come. Your confidence is a reflection of the healing, growth, and resilience you've cultivated throughout this journey. It's built on the foundation of self-worth and the belief in your abilities to overcome challenges. Walking in this confidence means stepping into each day with assurance, knowing that you have the strength and tools to navigate whatever comes your way. Each obstacle is now an opportunity to reaffirm your worth, and each step forward is a testament to the progress you've made.

This newfound confidence will continue to shape how you approach your future. It will guide your decisions, impact your relationships, and inspire those around you. As you move forward, embrace the power of this confidence, trusting that it will lead you toward new opportunities and a life aligned with your values and goals. Remember that confidence is not about never doubting yourself, but about how you rise in those moments with grace and perseverance. Let this confidence be your compass, empowering you to face the future with courage, clarity, and conviction.

Workbook Lesson: Day 29 - Maintaining Momentum

Sustaining Your Growth: Keeping the Momentum Alive

Maintaining momentum in your healing journey is vital for ensuring that the growth you've achieved continues to flourish. The progress you've made is the result of your dedication, reflection, and commitment to becoming your best self. To keep this momentum, it's essential to stay consistent in the habits and practices that have brought you to this point. Whether it's daily self-care, setting healthy boundaries, or regularly reflecting on your personal goals, these actions will reinforce your progress. As *Philippians 3:14* reminds us, *"I press on toward the goal to win the prize for which God has called me heavenward in Christ Jesus."* This verse is a powerful reminder to keep pressing forward with faith and purpose.

To sustain this forward motion, it's important to embrace flexibility. Life will inevitably bring changes, and some of these shifts may challenge your sense of stability. Rather than viewing these changes as setbacks, see them as opportunities to apply the resilience and confidence you've cultivated. Each challenge is a moment to reaffirm your self-worth and to practice the lessons you've learned along the way. By celebrating even the smallest victories, you acknowledge the significance of your journey and remind yourself that healing is not about perfection but about progress.

Finally, staying connected to your support system and practicing self-compassion are key in maintaining momentum. There will be days when progress feels slow, but leaning on those who encourage you and showing yourself grace in moments of struggle will help you stay on track. Remember, this journey is a marathon, not a sprint, and with each step, you are moving closer to the life of fulfillment and purpose that you are building. Trust in the path ahead and know that God is walking beside you every step of the way, guiding you toward continued healing and growth.

Purpose:

This lesson is about learning how to sustain your healing progress and prevent setbacks. By maintaining momentum, you can continue to grow without losing sight of your goals.

Introduction:

Healing is not a linear process, and there will be times when it feels easier or harder to stay on track. The key is to keep the momentum going, even during difficult moments.

Reflection Exercise:

1. Identify one challenge that might cause you to lose momentum.

Journal Prompt: What specific challenge could disrupt your progress, and how can you prepare yourself to handle it with resilience?

---

2. Reflect on the daily habits or practices that have been most beneficial in maintaining your growth. Think about how you can continue or adapt these practices to support your healing in the future.

   Journal Prompt: What habits have most supported your growth, and how will you integrate them into your life moving forward?

Reflection Question

How can you stay motivated and committed to your growth even when progress feels slow, or setbacks occur?

Journal Prompt: Reflect on the steps you can take to stay dedicated to your healing journey. What will help you remain focused and positive, even during challenging times?

_____

_____

_____

Day 29 – Conclusion: Pressing Forward with Faith and Resilience

As you come to the close of this lesson, remember that maintaining momentum is not about perfection but about persistence. The progress you've made is the result of consistent effort, reflection, and a deep commitment to your healing journey. To keep moving forward, it's essential to continue practicing the habits that have supported your growth—whether it's daily self-care, setting boundaries, or taking time to reflect on your goals. *Philippians 3:14* encourages us to, ***"press on toward the goal to win the prize for which God has called me heavenward in Christ Jesus."*** This scripture is a reminder that the journey requires perseverance and faith, and that each step you take brings you closer to the person you're becoming.

As life presents challenges, embrace flexibility and view these moments as opportunities to apply the strength and resilience you've developed. Even when progress feels slow, lean on your support network and practice self-compassion. Celebrate your victories, no matter how small, and trust that with each new day, you are moving closer to a life of purpose and fulfillment. Remember that God is walking with you through every step of this journey, providing the guidance and strength you need to stay on the path of healing and continued growth.

Workbook Lesson: Day 30 - Your New Steps Forward

Embracing a Future of Growth and Possibility

As you reach this pivotal moment in your healing journey, it's time to embrace the new steps forward that will continue to shape your path. Every step you've taken so far has laid the foundation for your growth, teaching you resilience, self-worth, and confidence. Now, as you move forward, the next phase will focus on integrating the lessons you've learned into your daily life. These new steps reflect your commitment to ongoing healing and the desire to reach your highest potential, with each step representing a deepened understanding of yourself and your capabilities. As *Psalm 37:23* reminds us, *"The Lord makes firm the steps of the one who delights in Him."* Trust that God is guiding your every step as you walk confidently into the future.

Your new steps forward include setting clear and purposeful intentions for what lies ahead. Whether you're continuing to build on the goals you've set, creating new habits, or releasing lingering fears from the past, each decision you make now paves the way for lasting change. It's essential to approach these new steps with confidence, but also with the flexibility to adjust when life's challenges arise. The self-awareness and strength you've developed equip you to navigate these challenges with grace, knowing that you are capable of overcoming whatever comes your way.

As you move into this new chapter, take a moment to celebrate how far you've come. Reflect on the personal growth you've experienced, the obstacles you've overcome, and the strength you've discovered within yourself. Your new steps forward are not just about moving ahead—they are about owning your journey, trusting your instincts, and stepping into the future with renewed hope and purpose. Continue nurturing your self-worth, seek new opportunities, and remain committed to the ongoing process of healing and self-discovery. Every step forward is a testament to your courage and the extraordinary journey you are on.

Purpose:

Today's focus is on committing to your next steps in the journey of healing and self-worth. Reflect on your accomplishments and visualize your future with clarity and purpose.

Introduction:

You've come a long way in your healing journey, but this is just the beginning. As you move forward, it's essential to take time to reflect on what you've accomplished and envision the path ahead.

Reflection Exercise:

1. Take a moment to reflect on the biggest challenges you've overcome during this journey. Think about the ways in which you've grown stronger, more resilient, and more aligned with your true self.

   Journal Prompt: What have been the most significant lessons learned from overcoming these challenges, and how will they shape your next steps?

   _____

   _____

   _____

2. Spend a few minutes visualizing the future you're working toward. Picture yourself living in alignment with

your self-worth, goals, and values, and think about the daily actions that will bring this vision to life.

Journal Prompt: What steps will you take each day to continue nurturing your growth and stay committed to your long-term goals?

Reflection Question

How will you ensure that each new step forward reflects the growth and resilience you've cultivated throughout this journey?

Journal Prompt: Write down how your future decisions and actions will embody the confidence, self-worth, and purpose you've developed, and what practices will keep you aligned with these values.

_____

_____

_____

Day 30 – Conclusion: Stepping Boldly Into the Future with Confidence

As you conclude this final lesson, take a moment to reflect on how far you've come in your journey of healing and growth. Each step you've taken has not only strengthened your resilience but also deepened your understanding of your self-worth and potential. Now, as you prepare to move forward, your new steps represent a continuation of that growth, integrating the lessons you've learned into your everyday life. These steps, guided by purpose and intention, reflect your commitment to ongoing healing. As *Psalm 37:23* reminds us, *"The Lord makes firm the steps of the one who delights in Him."* Trust that God is with you, guiding your every move as you step confidently into the future.

Your journey doesn't end here; it's just the beginning of a new chapter filled with possibilities. As you set your intentions for the future—whether by setting new goals, creating healthy habits, or letting go of lingering fears—remember that you have the strength to navigate life's challenges. Celebrate the progress you've made and continue to nurture the self-worth and confidence that have brought you this far. With each new step, you are moving toward a life of purpose, fulfillment, and hope, knowing that God walks beside you in every moment. Keep pressing forward, trusting that the best is yet to come.

Activity:

Celebrating Your Growth and Charting Your New Steps Forward

Objective:

This final activity is designed to help you reflect on the progress you've made, celebrate your personal growth, and plan your new steps forward. By engaging with these exercises, you will create a powerful roadmap that solidifies your healing journey and propels you into a future of continued growth and resilience. Each part of this activity encourages self-reflection, intention setting, and a celebration of the progress you've made so far.

1: Reflecting on Your Journey (15 minutes)

Spend time reflecting on the significant changes and growth you've experienced throughout this healing process

> *Journal Prompt:* Write down your thoughts and feelings as you acknowledge how far you've come.

_____

_____

_____

Exercise:

What are three key lessons you've learned throughout your journey?

Journal Prompt:

_____

_____

_____

What challenges have you overcome, and how did those moments shape your resilience?

Journal Prompt:

_____

_____

_____

Take this moment to celebrate the inner strength you've developed. Reflect on how these lessons have helped transform your mindset and self-worth.

Step 2: Defining Your New Foundations (15 minutes)

Now that you've identified your growth, it's time to define the new foundations upon which you will continue to build your life. Consider your values, goals, and the practices that have helped you grow stronger.

Exercise:

1. What are the core values that will guide you as you move forward?

   Journal Prompt:

   _____

   _____

   _____

2. What daily practices will you continue to maintain to nurture your self-worth and resilience?

   Journal Prompt:

_____

_____

_____

By defining your new foundations, you create a solid base upon which to build a future aligned with your true self.

Step 3: Setting Your New Goals (20 minutes)

Setting long-term goals is essential to staying focused on the future you want to create. These goals should reflect the growth you've experienced and your commitment to continued healing.

Exercise:

1. What are two long-term goals you want to achieve in the next six months? Consider goals that align with your emotional, spiritual, or personal development.

   Journal Prompt:

_____

_____

_____

2. Break these long-term goals into smaller, actionable steps you can begin working on immediately.

By creating a clear plan, you empower yourself to continue building upon the progress you've made.

Journal Prompt:

_____

_____

_____

Step 4: Visualization of Your New Steps (10 minutes)

Close your eyes and visualize yourself taking the new steps forward. Imagine the life you want to create, filled with confidence, resilience, and self-worth.

Exercise:

1. **Visualization Prompt**: Picture yourself six months from now, living out your goals. What does your day look like? How do you feel? What are the positive changes you notice in yourself?

   Journal Prompt:

   _____

   _____

   _____

This visualization will help solidify your commitment to the journey ahead and inspire you to keep moving forward with purpose.

Step 5: Commit to Your Future (5 minutes)

It's time to commit to the new steps you will take moving forward. By writing down your commitment, you solidify your intention to continue growing and healing.

Exercise:

1. Write a letter to yourself, committing to the next phase of your healing journey. Include the goals you've set, the resilience you've built, and the new foundations you've created.

   Journal Prompt:

   _____

   _____

   _____

Reflection Question: How will the new foundations you've built continue to support your growth and resilience in the future?

   Journal Prompt:

_____

_____

_____

This final activity encourages you to reflect on your progress and commit to the steps that will lead you toward a life rooted in confidence, resilience, and purpose. Celebrate how far you've come and step forward into your future with hope and strength.

Conclusion for Chapter 4: New Steps: What Is Yours?

As you come to the end of this book, it's important to pause and reflect on the immense progress you've made in your healing journey. You've taken steps to uncover your true worth, strengthen your resilience, and let go of past burdens that no longer serve you. Each chapter has been a building block, guiding you through self-reflection, setting boundaries, and embracing the healing process with intention. You've learned to cultivate self-compassion, rewrite your inner dialogue, and commit to long-term growth that aligns with the person you are becoming.

The journey ahead will undoubtedly hold new challenges, but now, you are equipped with the tools and inner strength to navigate them with grace and confidence. The foundations you've built are strong, rooted in self-worth and resilience, allowing you to approach each new step with purpose and clarity. Whether it's setting long-term goals, embracing new opportunities, or maintaining the momentum you've created, you now have a clear path forward. You can trust that the journey of healing and growth is ongoing, but you are prepared to walk it with unwavering courage and conviction.

As you continue to chart your path forward, remember that this is only the beginning of a lifelong process of self-discovery and healing. Each step you take is a testament to your strength and commitment to living a life filled with purpose, confidence, and resilience. Continue nurturing your self-worth, celebrating your growth, and leaning into the new foundations you've built. The future is yours to shape, and with every step, you are becoming the person you were meant to be.

Weekly Prayer for Chapter 4: New Steps – Charting Your Path Forward

Heavenly Father,

As I enter this final chapter of my healing journey, I thank You for guiding me every step of the way. You have shown me my worth, strengthened my resilience, and given me the courage to let go of the past. I ask for Your continued guidance as I embrace the new foundations You are helping me build. Give me the wisdom to discern my next steps and the faith to trust in the future You have planned for me.

Lord, as I move forward, I pray that You fill my heart with confidence and peace. Help me to remain rooted in Your love and to trust that each step I take is guided by Your purpose. Let me walk in the strength of the foundations I've built, knowing that with You by my side, I am equipped for the path ahead. May every new opportunity and challenge I face reflect the person You are shaping me to be.

In Jesus' name, I pray. Amen.

Continuing Your Journey with These Resources

Explore a variety of tools designed to support your healing, growth, and transformation:

Website: www.journeysofwomenministries.net

Books and eBooks are available on website and Amazon

- Hope Victory Over Darkness

- Workbook: 30-Day Guide to Healing and Building Self-Worth

- Family and Friends Support Toolkit

- Am I Damaged Goods: A 30-Day Guide to Restoring Your Heart, Mind, and Spirit from Trauma of Abuse

- Childlike Fath: Discovering The Father, The Son, and The Holy Spirit (Release Date 12/01/2024)

- Here Me: A Voice Not Hear, Echoes of Silence (Release Date 01/01/2025)

- The Forgotten: Voices Silenced, Those Whom Time Forgot (Release Date 01/20/2025)

Workbooks:

- Workbook: 30-Day Guide to Healing and Building Self-Worth

- Am I Damaged Goods: A 30-Day Guide to Restoring Your Heart, Mind, and Spirit from Trauma of Abuse

- Family and Friends Support Toolkit

eBooks: PDF or Kindle

- Hope Victory Over Darkness

- A 30-Day Guide to Healing and Building Self-Worth

- Am I Damaged Goods: A 30-Day Guide to Restoring Your Heart, Mind, and Spirit from Trauma of Abuse

- Family and Friends Support Toolkit

- Childlike Fath: Discovering The Father, The Son, and The Holy Spirit (Release Date 12/01/2024)

- Here Me: A Voice Not Heard: Echoes of Silence (Release Date 01/01/2025)

- The Forgotten: Voices Silenced, Those Whom Time Forgot (Release Date 01/20/2025)

Journals:

- The Healing Journal: A 30-Day Guide to Healing and Building Self-Worth (Release Date 11/23/2024)

- The Healing Journal: Family and Friends Support Toolkit (Release Date 12/10/2024

- The Healing Journal: "Am I Damaged Goods" A 30-Day Guide to Restoring Your Heart, Mind, and Spirit from Trauma of Abuse (Release Date 11/15/2024)

- The Healing Journal: Childlike Fath Discovering The Father, The Son, and The Holy Spirit (Release Date 12/23/2024)

- The Healing Journal: My Letters to Me Release Date 01/01/2025)

Free and Paid Online Courses

- New Mind Set: New Results Release Date 12/01/2024

- Am I Damaged Goods? (Release Date 11/23/2024

- Bible Studies (Coming Soon 01/01/2025)

Note: More to Come

All Books, eBooks, Workbooks, and Journals are or will be available on Journeys of Women Ministries website and Amazon

Visit www.journeysofwomenministries.net to learn more and access these resources. Your journey to healing, hope, and renewal continues here—explore these tools and take the next step today.

Made in the USA
Columbia, SC
29 November 2024

46701024R00137